Rafael Epstein is an awarding-winning journalist and ABC radio broadcaster. He currently presents *Drive* on 774 ABC Melbourne. He has won two Walkley Awards—his first with *The Age's* Nick McKenzie for their reporting on police corruption during Melbourne's underworld wars, his second for his coverage of the arrest of Mohammed Hanif, the Indian-born doctor falsely accused over his connections to the failed bombings in London and Glasgow in 2007. Epstein has worked for the ABC in news and current affairs in Sydney, Melbourne, Canberra, Timor, Indonesia, Europe and the Middle East. He has also worked in the Investigative Unit at *The Age*, focusing on Australia's special forces and their role in Afghanistan.

He knew Ben Zygier when they were both involved in Jewish youth movements in Melbourne.

PRISONER X

RAFAEL EPSTEIN

MELBOURNE
UNIVERSITY
PRESS

MELBOURNE UNIVERSITY PRESS
An imprint of Melbourne University Publishing Limited
11–15 Argyle Place South, Carlton, Victoria 3053, Australia
mup-info@unimelb.edu.au
www.mup.com.au

First published 2014
Text © Rafael Epstein, 2014
Design and typography © Melbourne University Publishing Limited, 2014

Cover design by Sandy Cull
Typeset by Megan Ellis
Printed in Australia by McPherson's Printing Group

National Library of Australia Cataloguing-in-Publication entry

Epstein, Rafael, author.
Prisoner X/Rafael Epstein.

9780522864403 (paperback)
9780522864410 (ebook)

Zygier, Ben.
  Jews, Australian—Israel—Biography.
  Australians—Israel—Biography.
  Prisoners—Death.
  Intelligence service—Israel.
  Espionage, Israeli.
327.125694

This project has been assisted by the Australian Government through the Australia Council, its principal arts funding and advisory body.

CONTENTS

Contents

Contents

AUTHOR'S NOTE

Reporters who try to uncover espionage enter a journalistic hall of mirrors, where you can only see what you already know, or what other people want you to see. In such investigations, answers can only be found when you ask the right questions, and very few facts are verifiable.

Discovering precisely what Ben Zygier did, dealing with agencies whose raison d'être is to deceive, has not been easy. I spoke to national security sources in Australia and Israel, and to members of Ben's family and his friends. I also accessed the court records that were first sought by Israel's *Ha'aretz* newspaper, among others, and relied on works on the Mossad by journalists in Israel. This book represents my best effort to explain what happened. My research suggests that much of what has been published previously about Ben has not been accurate. Over the coming years, more accounts of his life may be produced and they may verify what I have been told, though they could also prove me wrong.

There are many people in Israel and Australia who would vehemently oppose the publication of this book. I know that any further publicity about Ben's life will especially pain his family and friends, and I am truly sorry I have added to that, but there are vitally important questions about Ben's story that are still unanswered. I have changed the names of some of the people whose lives were intertwined with Ben's, including those of his wife and his eldest daughter. And I have chosen to not divulge certain details to protect the identities of some people who spoke with me for this book. But Ben's story is already public, and the portrayal of him as either a zealot or a traitor is not only wrong, it covers up the lack of transparency and simple care displayed by the governments of Australia and Israel. Ben's fate ended up affecting the relationship between the two countries, and it also affected perceptions of Australia's Jewish community. And as intelligence agencies play a crucial role in both societies, they also need scrutiny. I have devoted my professional life to the principles of transparency, and to the revelation of facts that could help to ensure governments and their agencies are as open as they can be with the people they serve, and it is in this vein that I have written this book.

While grappling for solid truths about Ben's life, I kept in mind the motto of the agency for which he worked. The Mossad's full name is Ha Mossad le Modi'in ule Tafkidim Meyuḥadim. Its direct translation is 'the Institute for Intelligence and Special Operations', which is usually shortened to 'the Institute'. But translating its motto is not as simple, and that reflects much about the organisation's true nature. The motto 'Where there is no counsel, the people fall, but where there are many counsellors there is safety' is taken from the Book of Proverbs. In the King James Bible, the Hebrew word *takhbulot* is the basis for the words 'counsel' and 'counsellors'. But in modern spoken Hebrew, *takhbulot* is understood to mean something very different—ploys or a batch of tricks. Even in the Bible, *takhbulot* is not always translated as 'counsel'. For example, in the phrase 'for by *takhbulot* thou shalt make thy war', it is often interpreted as 'ruses'.[1]

This suggests another way to translate the Mossad's motto: 'Without ruses, Israel would fall, but when there is plenty of misinformation, Israel finds salvation.' This motto is worth remembering when trying to work out how much of what has been said about Ben Zygier's life is verifiable and how much is speculation.

A DARK DAY

'This is Ayalon prison … Listen! He hanged himself. We need an ambulance!' These are the first words uttered by the guard of the mystery prisoner when he calls the paramedics. The warden has just walked into cell 15 and found the man hanging immobile in his shower. As he calls for an ambulance, other prison guards remove the wet sheet that is twisted around the prisoner's neck and tied to the window in the bathroom/shower area at the back of his cell. 'I don't have details,' the warden insists over the phone. 'I'll tell the medic to get back to you.'[1] It is 8.20 p.m. on Wednesday 15 December 2010. For the entire ten months that the inmate has been with them, the guards in the Israeli prison have not known his name, what he has been charged with, or that he used to work for Israel as a spy.

The wardens soon realise their attempts to resuscitate the prisoner are futile. His body is cool and there is no pulse. Even to their untrained eyes, it looks like he has been dead for some time. It should not be easy to kill yourself inside one of the most watched

1

solitary cells in Israel, a cell with three cameras trained on it. But these are only useful if the images they broadcast are crisp and clean, and such images are only as reliable as the guards who watch them. The cameras have needed replacing for months, and on this night their blurry images were not being watched.

Ayalon prison, Israel's biggest, is a rambling collection of imposing sheds covered in corrugated iron, faceless multistorey buildings, massive brick walls and forbidding fences. Lengths of razor wire are coiled lazily on top of each other; they drip off parapets and climb up the guard towers like metal ivy. The medical base sits just a few hundred metres away, its ambulances parked behind a low metal fence. Within minutes of the guard's call the paramedics are inside the prison's reinforced brick and metal walls, but they're bewildered by the lack of information. The paramedics are not told the prisoner's name; they're not shown a photo of him; they're not told his birthdate; they're not given other basic details like next of kin. The guards refer to the man only as Prisoner X, or *ploni*, the Hebrew equivalent of John Doe. The paramedics are confused by this but are told to carry on. 'The jail doesn't give us any details about this man, nothing, not his ID number, nothing at all,' one ambulance officer complains on the night. 'This is a crazy cell. I've never seen anything like this, cameras everywhere.'[2]

Before the body is moved from the cell, the ambulance officers are ordered out and the guards are instructed to leave their supervision room next door. Plain-clothes intelligence officers swoop into the cell to ensure the mystery prisoner has left no last-minute communication that may reveal why he has been held in such tight security. They find nothing.

As the prisoner's body is wheeled on a trolley to the outer reaches of the jail, the guards and ambulance officers finally learn his name. At first they're told that it is Ben Alon, but minutes later the surname is changed to Zygier. Ben had been born into the Zygier family in suburban Melbourne. But four years before his death, he and his wife Haya had chosen a new surname—Alon—to signify the beginning of their married life in Israel.

2

To the guards, Ben was a mystery. But even to those who did know him, he presented contradictions. 'He had some dark days,' one of his friends told me. 'And who knows, maybe you wake up one day and you just don't see an exit.'

‹ ›

At 11 a.m. on the day of Ben's death, his wife Haya presents herself at the entrance to Ayalon with their five-month-old daughter on her hip. They endure the security ritual that has become depressingly familiar over this remarkably horrible year of Haya's life. Her ordeal began with Ben's arrest at the end of January and continues with the burden of security officials trailing her to and from their home in one of Israel's nicer commuter suburbs, near Tel Aviv. Haya fears that every call she makes is listened to, and she knows she is closely observed whenever she visits her husband.

Ten minutes after their arrival, a junior intelligence officer shows Haya and her baby into Ben's cell. Haya and her husband begin to talk, but after a while the conversation deteriorates into an argument. Her news is devastating: she is leaving him. The pressure of his imprisonment, the allegations against him and the need to keep her turmoil hidden have all taken their toll. Ben has eagerly anticipated another visit from the daughter he is only ever to see inside his cell—and he is not prepared for Haya's demand for a divorce. Instead, with winter approaching, he's written a list of clothes he wants Haya to bring on her next visit.

After nearly an hour, with Ben edgy, upset and in tears, Haya and her daughter leave the cell. It is only after she's left that Ben remembers the list. But the junior intelligence officer refuses to call Haya back and give the note to her—it is a breach of the rules. Ben's response is immediate and furious: he rips the note to pieces to make clear his anger. Haya hears her husband's howls of anguish. She wants to try to calm him down. It is an indication of how strictly Ben's life is regulated that it takes an 'exceptional' bending of the rules for Haya to be given permission to re-enter the cell. When she leaves for a second time just a few minutes later, she too is crying.

Ben is far from calm after seeing Haya, but the guards and the social worker assigned to look after him decide he is no more upset than normal. He is often in tears after family visits.

Within an hour, Ben calls his mother Louise in Melbourne. They have always been close and speak regularly. When Ben was younger they were 'on the phone to each other several times a day', says one close observer of the family. Even while living in Israel, first as a member of its army, then as a lawyer in Tel Aviv and later while working as a spy in Europe, Ben always kept in touch with his mother. Since he has been in jail, Louise has travelled regularly from Australia to visit and help with his lawyers.

Louise is distraught after Ben's phone call. Sometime after 2 p.m., she sends an email to her son's lawyer, Moshe Mazur, one of the few people who knows the details of Ben's supposed crimes (he has yet to disclose them). She writes that she is worried because Haya is leaving Ben. She fears he will try to kill himself with an overdose of sleeping pills. Clearly alarmed by what he has read, in the middle of the afternoon the lawyer makes an unusual phone call to the prison: when he is told Ben is asleep, Mazur demands he be woken up. Ben soon calls him and they speak for nearly an hour. The prison guards do not record Mazur's concerns, nor his call with Ben, so there is no direct record of the prisoner's mood after he has spoken with his lawyer.

‹ ›

Guards in towers are watching over the perimeter of the prison, scanning its surroundings. These include new apartment blocks, a rundown shopping centre and a massive telecommunications building bristling with antennae. Some of the towers have cameras trained over the adjacent roads, and the pictures they record are fed back to the prison's command centre, where four guards watch TV screens on a big desk. More images are projected onto additional screens higher up on the wall in front of the guards, which they can see by lifting their heads. The guards can scan images from hundreds of cameras around the high-security facility, including those inside cell 15. But the technology is faulty, providing fuzzy images when the lights in the cells are on and even less-clear pictures at night when the lights are switched off.

It is the responsibility of a lowly ranked master sergeant to use the cameras to check on Ben every half-hour. He is meant to monitor the images from the guardroom adjacent to cell 15. At 5.52 p.m., the master sergeant makes a note in a logbook that the prisoner is calm and then he leaves the guardroom. The man is straying from routine, but there are no written orders regarding what the guards must do with this mystery prisoner.

On this night, the master sergeant makes three crucial mistakes. His first is to leave the guardroom after noting Ben's calmness— he is supposed to stay there until 10 p.m. each night. The second is that when he heads to the command centre, he forgets to take with him the logbook in which he records his half-hourly checks on the prisoner. He later says that despite the lack of evidence in the logbook, he continued to check on Ben via the cameras.

The third mistake would have been apparent after Ben entered the bathroom. If the master sergeant had been watching the remote camera feeds in the command centre, he would not have been able to see Ben's final moments. The camera that gave a view of the shower could only be watched from the guardroom because its link to the command centre was broken. For some months, the guards had known that while the cell's other two cameras could be watched remotely, they could only observe Ben's bathroom when they were next door to his cell.

The master sergeant later records a devastating admission: 'Had the guardroom been manned at the time of the event and before it, and had the cameras been in order, I would surely have noticed Zygier's preparations for his suicide, and prevented it.'

‹ ›

At 6.05 p.m., watched by the cameras in his cell, Ben turns off the light and then puts a chair next to his bed. On the chair he places a sheet that he has torn into two pieces. Fidgeting in bed, he must know that what he is contemplating will devastate his parents and leave his children without a father. Clearly he is desperate. He has spent ten months in Israel's maximum-security jail. He was distressed to miss the birth of his second daughter five months earlier, and in November he had been absent from his elder daughter's birthday. Ben gets up and turns on his small TV. But he appears agitated and cannot keep calm. He turns the TV off within minutes and lies in bed.

At 6.54 p.m., Ben again gets up off his bed and turns on the TV, then goes into the bathroom cubicle. His cell is mostly dark, but some of the glare from the TV spills into the bathroom through the translucent door. The cameras are designed to pick up movement in the dark using a poorly functioning infra-red lamp, so the images of the inside of the shower cubicle are dim but discernible to a close observer. For more than twenty minutes, the camera tape shows Ben standing in the shower cubicle.

‹ ›

At 8 p.m. in the command centre, for some reason he has never shared, the master sergeant decides something is not quite right. He sends a more junior warden to check on Prisoner X. Thirteen minutes later, after an unhurried walk, the junior warden enters the empty guardroom and presses the button on the intercom to communicate with Ben. There is no response from the prisoner. The junior guard doesn't enter the cell. Instead, he calls the master sergeant on his radio and asks him to come and check on the prisoner himself.

The master sergeant reaches the guardroom six minutes later, switches on the cell's light and steps inside. He immediately looks through the transparent door at the back of the cell that leads to the bathroom. Prisoner X is slumped in the shower stall, his chest visible but unmoving—Ben's limp body is being kept upright by the sheet coiled around his neck.

A family friend asks me later, 'He thought he was under CCTV. Did he realise he would succeed?' It is a common thought among Ben's friends, who believe he may have overestimated just how closely he was being watched.

‹ ›

Because Ben's jailing was a highly protected state secret, during his incarceration he had been discouraged from talking to the guards. His social workers and psychiatrists knew a little more about his case, but those conversations were limited too, because by court order Ben could not discuss the charges against him. He could speak about them only with his lawyer, but when he did, he did not broach his inner turmoil. His conversations were similar to the walks he would take in the small yard next door to his cell. He could walk as much as he wanted to, but he was confined to pacing alone behind high metal walls, never seeing another prisoner. Kept under what one of the country's senior judges later described as 'the utmost level of secrecy', he was rarely able to speak openly.

In the last ten months of his life, there had been many warning signs of Ben's failing mental health, and at least one instance of self-harm. Over that period, Ben had been examined by four psychiatrists and two doctors. This is a typical example of their terse summaries: 'Mental state: abnormal findings, depression, deteriorated mood, has trouble sleeping, wakes up early, poor appetite, dispirited, tearfulness.' His guards later said that they saw Ben deteriorate physically: 'He became just a pair of eyes … he barely ate.'

Many who knew Ben speak of a history of mental health problems before he went into prison, including a troubled relationship with eating, denying himself food on occasion. There were a number of deaths that had deeply affected him. At the end of 1995, while on holiday in Egypt, he had befriended a couple who a short time later died in a car accident. And two years later, dozens of his army friends died in one of the worst chopper crashes in Israel's military history. In the years before his arrest, he visited a psychiatrist and was diagnosed with an anxiety disorder. In the month before his death, he told the prison psychiatrist that he'd twice tried to kill himself several years previously. Ben's parents and wife knew these things, yet it seems that the Mossad either hadn't uncovered his mental fragility or had decided it was a factor that could be successfully managed.

Despite the tragedy that befell Ben, many of the men who were in his life have asked themselves whether they too would have joined Israel's elite intelligence service if they'd had the chance. 'He lived the dream in one sense,' says a family friend. Like Ben, many Jewish boys are brought up on stories of the exploits of Israel's soldiers and spies. It's common for thirteen-year-old boys to receive as bar mitzvah presents books about the heroic soldiers who fought in the Six-Day War in June 1967, and thrilling tales of Mossad spies as the protectors and avenging angels of a defiant nation.

One of Ben's friends told me, 'Who knows what you or I would do? You get offered a chance to be 007 or Harrison Ford, and when an opportunity comes, you take it.'

BOY

The Ben I Knew

When I first met Ben he was a blue-eyed boy in primary school in Melbourne, with curly hair and an easygoing but mischievous smile. It was 1987, and for two hours every Sunday afternoon, he and his friends were my responsibility as I made my first, faltering high-schooler attempts to be a youth leader. Ben, meanwhile, had his first taste of the boredom and the exhilaration that is part of a unique Jewish subculture.

I have a photo of Ben from this time, sitting on the ground, his head leaning heavily on his hand as he looks quizzically over his shoulder at the camera. It is the same smile and blue eyes that stare out from the photo of Ben flashed around the world's media two years after his death, when the identity of Prisoner X was finally made public. This young boy in my photo is crouching over a black plastic bag, which must be part of some long-forgotten game played on an idle afternoon.

I remember Ben distinctly as a cheeky, warm, quietly spoken boy who would only get loud when he was sparked by his friends. As a teenager, I could not have understood what the passage of time would bring. The longer the kids were in youth movements, the more serious and ideological they became. By Year 12 most were committed to a year in Israel after school and then another few years back in Australia, leading kids just as I had mentored Ben. Few of us ended up living in Israel, and even fewer of us ended up in the Israeli army for anything more than the bare minimum of national service. I could never have imagined that one of the friendly kids in my care would one day make the significant decision to go and live in Israel and end up working as a spy.

Ben spent a few years with our Zionist youth movement, which was called Netzer. We met each week in the leafy grounds of a grand old colonial mansion in Armadale. In the 1970s the building had become The King David School, and it was here that Ben also came during the week for his regular schooling. Through Melbourne's wet winters and scalding summers, Ben was one of the twenty or thirty kids who came every weekend to our youth group. They didn't know that our lacklustre, poorly planned games were the last remnants of a fiery intellectual and political ferment that had bounced out of late nineteenth-century Europe. Back then, Zionist youth movements were part of the beginning of the Jewish brand of nationalism. Nearly a hundred years later in Australia, for most of us, Zionist movements were just a bit of fun on a weekend afternoon.

Youth-movement kids are different from the rest of the Jewish community, though. As they progress through high school they become more ideological, more interested in social justice and more likely to be passionate about politics in Australia, as well as in Israel. Few of the people who spent substantial time in movements came out with anything other than a idealistic view of a way the world should be remade, but not everyone who felt like that at the time ended up taking action in the real world, like working in politics, or moving to Israel.

Lazing under the bough of a tree in the grounds of King David, my biggest challenge was fighting to keep kids like Ben and his friends more focused on Jewish history than on a water bomb fight or the other games they'd rather be playing. My fellow Netzer *madrichim* (youth leaders) and I had to come up with fun, casual activities, art projects and discussions that we could lace with the odd educational strand of Jewish content, such as Israeli history. I remember playing a game where two teams were each given three tennis balls and then had to steal each other's balls—one side took on the identity of heroic Jewish pioneers setting up 'illegal' farms in 1930s Palestine, while the other side was filled with 'baddies', British soldiers who were trying to stop the settlers.

Each session began with the singing of the Israeli national anthem. Netzer's quiet, amiable Jewish liberalism was entwined with the belief that we should all consciously make a decision to go and live in Israel. That is what Zionism was supposed to mean. As a sixteen-year-old I knew this was rarely acted on, but I was happy to teach the accepted ideology. In hindsight, the ideology wasn't nearly as important to me as the idea of deliberately and provocatively self-empowering kids. The joy I'd experienced in coming into my own sense of who I was, under the care of people just a few years older than me, was something I wanted to pass on to kids like Ben.

On paper, organising weekly administrative meetings, helping out at a synagogue and meeting kids from other youth movements can look mundane. But to me, it was those kids who only went to regular school who were missing out. I was the one who was finding out what life was really all about. Each weekday at school felt like a life lived in black and white, whereas on the weekends— and sometimes on weeknights—the world was revealed to me in glorious technicolour. Netzer may have met in the drab grounds of a school and within the bland walls of a synagogue storage room, but at those get-togethers, political and personal passions seemed to bleed into one another. It was one of the best times of my life.

Describing a youth movement as a community group doesn't capture the ideologically soaked euphoria that can make it so intoxicating. Netzer was a place where making friends, meeting girls and boys, was actively encouraged; where exuberance, creativity and being opinionated made up the default personality; where a sense of social responsibility and ethical behaviour blended seamlessly with the worst excesses of teenage behaviour. That typical teenage feeling that the world really can be a better place was supercharged by the knowledge that people just like me, doing just what I was doing, had helped create the State of Israel forty years before.

As we get older, decades of our lives can be reduced to bare flashes of memory. I need to look at my photo albums to remember much more of Netzer than slices of summer and winter camps, meetings and day-long philosophical battles. At the time, it felt like some sacred flame of ideology that was passed from high school student to shy primary school kid. The more mundane reality I remember was one of arcane arguments over the relative merits of paper plates or kosher meat.

For children from the comfortable suburbs of Melbourne, as most of us were, our youth movement could be eye-opening. Young people were taught by their peers, so rebellion was an invigorating concept, not a dull lesson. Also, the belief that young Jewish people could 'change the world' came with the fierce ideological edge that this was only possible if you lived in Israel. Most of the children were not swayed by this message—they got bored and drifted away. But some, like Ben and me, for some unfathomable reason, stayed for years. We were part of the regular world around us, but we deliberately, sometimes provocatively, marked ourselves as being apart from it. Being committed, being part of a youth movement, necessarily meant priding ourselves on being different.

Belonging

In the early 1900s in the provincial towns of Poland, many Jews felt confined by the rigid rural existence their ancestors had lived for hundreds of years. It was the same in the sophisticated cities of Germany, where Jews feared that the adoption of a more secular identity wouldn't protect them from a resurgent anti-Semitism. At the same time, many European countries were experiencing a surge of nationalism. Jewish nationalism seemed like a natural response, emerging at the same time as the new scouting movements in Germany and Britain. Zionist youth movements were a way for younger Jews to engage with the broader mood sweeping the continent, the feeling that Europe was on the cusp of nationalist upheaval.

In rural Poland, my grandparents were part of a youth movement called Gordonia, named after the revered left-wing Jewish philosopher called A.D. Gordon. Amid the political discussions, Gordonia was both intensely practical and ideological. It taught young Jews how to build fences and plough fields while encouraging them to discuss the political philosophy that should underpin a new Jewish state. Such youth movements were also part of the informal network that helped Jews travel by ship to newly acquired plots of land in what was then called Palestine. In 1913, the vibrant cultural and political life of Europe's Jewish communities nurtured the emergence of yet another socialist group, Hashomer Hatzair. One hundred years later, one of its most famous graduates, Ben Zygier, would be revealed as a former Mossad spy.

For many Jews around the world, Zionism reached its high-water mark between the establishment of the State of Israel in 1948 and the Six-Day War in 1967. Zionism after this time was seen as a lesser creed. By the late 1980s, insults like 'armchair Zionist' were commonly tossed around during heated arguments, and talk of a 'post-Zionist' age was firmly rejected. But faded though it was, this Zionism was my path to a more intense political awareness. However, it inevitably made me more aware of the nuances and passions of politics, movements such as Zionism are not about abstract ideology. They're about personal action and change within small communities. It was a small step from the casual curriculum of a youth movement to the significant political activism of a life in Israel.

Even without the added edge of the 1960s counterculture, the youth movement we experienced in the 1980s was still a heady, almost aphrodisiacal mix of history and self-awareness. The fusion of intensely forged friendships and ever-present ideology could not be disentangled from the normal teenage experience of personal and intellectual discovery. I have vivid, emotional memories of animated late-night conversations about the precise path to a life lived to its full potential, preferably in Israel. The intense sense of belonging, being part of something 'important' and 'significant', was experienced within a wild and rollicking group of exuberant extroverts, witty jokers and bright thinkers. At its best it was, as a friend once said to me, 'like rocket fuel for the soul'. The sweaty communal climax came with Israeli singing and dancing on a Friday night. We'd gleefully turn to each other and joke that we didn't need alcohol because we were 'high on Zionism'. That ecstasy would be the spark for Ben's later decision to live in Israel.

His Father's Footsteps

Parents would drop off their children at Netzer in the school holidays for a week away from home, bags stuffed with warm clothes and lollies to be eaten by torchlight. As the children greeted each other excitedly next to a hired bus, the other youth leaders and I would reassure the parents about the welfare of their offspring. We'd spend the bus trip itself scribbling out a plan for the days ahead.

Through such excursions and other activities, movements like Netzer gave Jewish kids something to do, with the added hope that they might also pick up something about Judaism or Israel, a culture the children and their parents might otherwise have ignored. But the experience was different for Ben. A passion for Israel and responsibility to community were familiar themes in his family.

Both of his parents played central roles in Melbourne's tight-knit Jewish community. Ben's mother Louise was a significant volunteer and fundraiser for the Jewish Museum. She was seen as a steady hand, someone who'd put all her energy into a task. She was also a person with deep friendships in the Jewish community, forged over many years. Louise was always willing to give advice, though only when asked. She would share her experiences and vulnerabilities in the belief that being honest about your own weaknesses was a strength.

Ben's father Geoff was a self-made businessman whose personal journey was founded in belief. He was brought up in a regular, non-observant Jewish household. In his younger days, Geoff was a bit of a rebel—a 'long-haired hippy', says someone who knew him well. But with the birth of Ben in 1976 and a daughter four years later, Geoff became interested in the practices of an observant Jew. He began to develop a passion for the discipline dictated by the orthodox rules of Judaism. Geoff became what is known in Hebrew as *baal teshuvah*, which means 'master of the return'. This describes secular Jews who become very observant, far more interested in their religion than they were previously. It took many years, but over time, Geoff even lost the interest in rock and roll that he had shared with his brother. Willy Zygier had found fame as the musical and personal partner of singer-songwriter Deborah Conway. Willy had musical talent, so his passion became his profession. But that wasn't the path chosen by Geoff. He ran the family business manufacturing breakfast cereal and other foods.

When Ben and his sister were children, Geoff's devotion created some tension in the family home. 'I think Louise found it difficult, and it was not in sympathy with how she felt about Judaism,' a family friend tells me. It's not unheard of in Jewish families for one member to become fastidiously more observant than everyone else in the household. In terms of keeping kosher, that can mean buying special food and using separate crockery and kitchen utensils for foods containing either milk or meat. It's a logistical exercise as much as a belief. 'I don't know if she believed or not,' says the friend. 'She was tolerant of it, but she found it hard.'

His discipline led to Geoff wearing a skullcap and the ritual fringes beneath his shirt known as *tzitzit*. He became *shomrei Shabbat*, which translates as 'guarding the Sabbath'. It meant that on Friday night and for most of Saturday, he consciously avoided anything that may be construed as work. 'It was not just *shomrei Shabbat*,' continues the friend. 'It was much deeper than that, and he changed—Geoff really changed.'

Importantly, Geoff's devotion to his religion and his community was an example for Ben to follow. Geoff sold the family business and in subsequent years he held important positions in the Jewish community, including roles at the Executive Council for Australian Jewry and the Jewish Community Council of Victoria. Running either organisation was like herding cats. Judaism is not a naturally hierarchical religion and the community is endlessly splintering into a variety of synagogues, affiliations and organisations—hence the cliché that when you put two Jews into the same room, you automatically get three opinions and four synagogues.

Keeping the community focused, and speaking with the one voice, was a triumph of Geoff's diplomacy and perseverance. He was warm and engaging, and he had a gift for talking that he passed on to his son—he could find something to say to anyone. This was perhaps one reason why Ben would later be thought of as suited to intelligence work.

But it wasn't just Geoff's accomplishments in his community that provided a template for Ben. In Geoff Zygier's world view, every person's actions were a reflection and product of personal belief, and those actions would be assessed and weighed by God. It was an approach he wrote about in community newsletters:

As always Torah [Bible] teaches us a major lesson: every mitzvah [commandment] must be performed even if inconsequential in our eyes because we don't know what is important to G-d,[1] or what the part may add to the whole. So when we undertake what some may consider trivial tasks, on occasion even chores, it must be remembered their importance is inestimable.

He was speaking on behalf of his community, but it was a sentiment familiar to those who knew him. Sometimes it could be a liberating view, but at other times it was a heavy burden, the constant testing of whether someone's actions adequately expressed their beliefs. However, it neatly dovetailed with the world view of a Zionist youth movement: leaders led by example.

None of Ben's close friends explicitly say it, but many imply that his Zionism was his way of emulating his father. Many see his devotion to Israel as a mirror image of his father's religious commitment. Going to live in Israel, following through on an ideology that many only talked about—these were familiar concepts to Ben.

Geoff also believed that what each Jew did as an individual reflected on the entire Jewish community. In 2006, when his son was working for Israeli intelligence in Europe, Geoff wrote in a community newsletter some prophetic words: 'Many believe that individual Jews constitute a corpus. Each Jew's success (or failure for that matter) reflects on all of us.'

STUDENT

Dance and Song

By 1990, Ben had switched from Netzer and its focus on progressive Judaism to the equally Zionist but more politically left-wing Hashomer Hatzair, or Hashy. I spent time with him in a clutch of different Zionist youth movements in Melbourne. We were part of a tight tribe-within-a-tribe inside the Jewish community. Ben was now an angular fifteen-year-old with long curly hair that he often pulled back into a ponytail. Sometimes raucous, he was an uplifting part of a small group of ideologically committed teenagers. My strongest memory of him during this period is of watching him amid a swirl of dancing people. He'd pulled the tie out of his hair and was shaking his head around, making silly faces and laughing uncontrollably. The rest of us danced around him, whatever he was saying drowned out by loud Israeli music.

His friends remember a diligent high school student with a fondness for outrageous jokes and crude stunts. Mostly, though, he was a gentle presence, clever and caring. To those who knew him casually, he was no more likely to go and live in Israel than any of his friends.

Like his uncle Willy, he liked to sing while strumming a guitar. 'We all would sit around playing guitar a lot. It was a nice thing to do,' says a friend, recalling one particularly warm summer evening spent on a nature strip somewhere in suburban Melbourne. He and Ben had both been to a party or a Hashy meeting at someone's house. Deborah Conway had just had a big hit with 'Release Me' and the friend remembers Ben teaching him how to string together the guitar chords for that song in a way that he couldn't have picked up by simply listening to it on the radio. 'I wouldn't have been able to work them out,' he tells me. 'The particular way to play them he would have learned from Willy, because it sounded exactly like the song.' The friend says it felt like Ben was sharing something special because he was Willy's nephew. Ben also gave him a recording of Willy and Deborah playing on the radio, laughing and chatting with each other and the interviewer.

'Release Me' was inspired by Conway's struggles with her record company, but when the friend heard about how Ben died, he felt that the first few lines of the song seemed equally pertinent to what had happened to Ben. The words echoed the faith Ben had once had in the nation he'd tried to serve.

Ben was seen by many of his high school friends as a sharing and thoughtful young man, even if he sometimes was a bit too keen to continue an argument. He was part of a happy group of ideological kids, and as their schooling came to an end they prepared for their youth-movement rite of passage—a year away in Israel.

A Magical Year Away

The stray cat hisses violently, startling me as I'm looking at the golden Dome of the Rock rising from the centre of the Old City of Jerusalem. Behind me, scattered under the low-hanging olive trees, is a large, fierce group of feral cats. They're clearly angry that I've invaded their space.

The public garden I'm standing in tumbles down the hill from a well-known promenade that looks north to Jerusalem's old ramparts and walls. This sweeping walkway provides one of the city's more spectacular views, and today, like most days, it is being visited by numerous tourists spilling from buses. I'm not here for the view, however. I'm here to visit Kiryat Moriah, which sits a few hundred metres back from the promenade.

Kiryat Moriah is a small collection of colleges where, like me in 1989 and Ben four years later, tens of thousands of young Jews have studied after high school as part of a year-long tour of Israel. Before we came here, Ben and I had been told that this place was special, that it would grant us the pinnacle experience of our young lives. It was not an exaggeration. During our year away, we each spent five months studying at Machon Le Madrechai Chutz La'Aretz—the Institute for Youth Leaders from Abroad. The exploits of those who've passed through the institute are the stuff of youth movement legend. These tales provide an important foundation for Zionist movements around the world.

My heart is pumping and my stomach is churning as I drive up to the building where I spent those vital months. I cry as I return for the first time in nearly a quarter of a century. I am overcome by a tumult of emotion and memories, sparked by minor things like the hideous ironwork that frames the dormitory windows. The memories must be deeply etched into my psyche because I've rarely experienced such an unexpected physical response to simply walking into a building.

Machon was a special cocktail of ideology and self-discovery. We were blissfully subsumed in an aphrodisiacal atmosphere. With an explosion of what felt like maturity, we became new people—our 'true selves'. It's not surprising, perhaps, to have such a formative experience straight after leaving the strict confines of high school. But Machon was a little different. We were far away from our parents for such a long time. For many, Machon was less an education and more a year-long party, and stories abound that are dominated by sex and alcohol. There was just enough adult supervision to ensure you were educated, fed and cared for, but not enough to stop you doing whatever you liked.

The connections I made with Israel and its people were no less real because I was a teenager, and those links would have been just as vivid and real for Ben. There was so much in the educational program that was genuinely illuminating and revelatory, and it all happened in a country that so easily enraptures and fascinates its visitors.

Machon sits within a small pocket of territory that came under Israeli control after the Six-Day War. It was not taken from Jordan, however, but rather was wrested from the UN, under which it had been a no-man's-land. It had contained a college for Palestinian girls from nearby villages, as well as an Israeli-run experimental farm. Following the war, more Israelis arrived to live here, and there is now a series of apartment blocks where once there was farmland.

Ostensibly, Machon is a place where young people come to learn how to help run the Zionist youth movements that send them to Israel in the first place. Over the past few decades, the Israeli Government has consistently reduced its subsidy for the program, so it is now almost as expensive to attend as another year of private school in Australia. But when I was sent here, it cost no more than $4000. It was a significant amount of money, yet it was a small price to pay for a year-long program that included several months on a kibbutz and stays in different parts of the country. Almost everyone who goes to Machon has spent several years in a youth movement looking forward to this magical year away. The lack of adult control, the sheer exuberance and fervour, only add to the sense of rebellion and participation in a very deep cause.

With the hot afternoon sun bouncing off the white stone buildings, I remember this addictive mix of hormones, history and the crazed joy of the cause. I wander around trying to work out where my bedroom was situated within the now-renovated buildings. I sit on a stone windowsill in one of the classrooms, which look the same as they did two decades ago when we went through that physical and intellectual ferment. I glance at the back wall and see a series of noticeboards covered in newspaper clippings. Pinned to one of the boards is a life-size cut-out of Ben Zygier's smiling face, taken from the pages of a glossy magazine. His bald head and blue eyes stare out at a classroom he almost certainly sat in himself years ago.

Aliyah

Ben returned from Israel in 1994 to become a *madrich*, teaching and looking after children in the same unremarkable, two-storey, cream-brick building in East St Kilda where he'd spent so many weekends during his own high school years. This was the home of the Melbourne branch of Hashomer Hatzair, established in 1953 in the heart of the city's Jewish enclave. The building is just a few hundred metres away from Carlisle Street, a shopping strip that used to be liberally sprinkled with Jewish shops and kosher butchers, some of which remain—you can still find kosher bakeries here that shut on Saturday.

Ben arrived back in Australia full of love for Israel, and he talked constantly about the possibility of going back to live there. 'He was very patriotic,' says someone who later worked with him. Another friend says that Ben would consistently tell him, 'I want to go to Israel. I want to go into the army.' It was especially unusual for someone from a left-wing movement like Hashy to be so keen on the army: participating in national service was one thing; a wish to enjoy the military life was another. This friend tells me, 'I almost felt obliged to show him the other side', to point out that there was an alternative to living in Israel. However, Ben 'was too far gone', the friend says, adding, 'It wasn't just *aliyah*.'

Aliyah, a fundamental tenet of Zionism, means 'ascent' and implies that a move to Israel is a move to a higher state of being. But Ben wanted even more than this. He didn't just want to move to Israel to continue the life he'd been living in Australia. He wanted to immerse himself in his new home, to prove himself there. One way in which he planned to do this was by completing more than the minimum service required for conscription into the Israeli army. Every eighteen-year-old born in Israel serves in the country's armed forces for three years, and new immigrants usually do a shortened form of this national service. But Ben wanted to serve for longer. He wanted to be far more than an average immigrant in his adopted country.

The inside of the somewhat shabby Hashy building in Melbourne displays a picture that spells out one of the foundation stories of Ben's youth movement. In the main hall is a large painting of a man called Mordechai Anielweiz, his open shirt revealing a muscular chest, a rock in his right hand. Anielweiz was the head of Hashy's Warsaw branch during World War II. He was at the heart of the Jewish resistance movement, inside the ghetto created by the Nazis in the Polish capital. This led to Anielweiz playing a key role in one of the most revered rebellions in Jewish history, the Warsaw Ghetto Uprising. The uprising culminated in the rebel leaders being forced to retreat to a house where they killed themselves rather than surrendering. The Nazis bulldozed the building, but the resulting pile of rubble was preserved. Many young Jews are now taken through the streets of Warsaw to that large knoll of earth, which rises up among the regular apartment blocks on a quiet avenue called Mila Street. It is a rite of passage for young Jews to stand on that grassy mound and light a candle in memory of the leaders of the uprising.

On other walls inside the Hashy building are many much smaller pictures, photos of the hundreds of people who have become part of Hashy's history in Melbourne—young boys and girls who have gone on to become farmers, authors, doctors, lawyers and political advisers. In the stairwell near the first floor, amid hundreds of other photos, is a small picture of a young high-schooler, Ben Zygier. His long curly hair is tied back tightly and he wears a Hashy camp T-shirt from 1988. He is watching an older Israeli man giving directions to a group of teenagers. The man's name is Akiva Viland, and he and his wife Rivka live on Kibbutz Gazit in northern Israel. This kibbutz became one of Ben's second homes in Israel, and Rivka turns out to be one of the few people who seem willing to speak openly to me about him.

Closing Ranks

I'm driving north from Tel Aviv along one of Israel's main freeways. This leg of my journey to try to understand Ben's past, which has seen me crisscross Israel in search of people who knew him well, takes me past some of the country's most desirable addresses, through places like Herziliya and Raanana. An hour into the drive, I veer east into the Galilee region and pass some of the Arab villages that dot the valley. This is one of the few places in Israel where you see billboards dominated by Arabic writing and surrounded by the minarets of mosques.

A short distance past these villages, I start to feel as though I am driving through part of Australia. Thick rows of gum trees line the road. I picture Ben travelling to Kibbutz Gazit on these same roads in the mid-1990s, visiting friends. If the impact of the heat didn't remind Ben of Australia, perhaps the winding roads and the eucalypts took him back there.

I arrive at the massive, well-resourced collective to find Rivka Viland nursing a slight cold. We sit in armchairs in her home, protected from the heat outside by the air conditioning. As she recounts what she remembers, she often looks not directly at me but at the sun-bleached garden beyond the windows.

Rivka is one of the few people who knew Ben in his final years of school in Australia and also later when he was in the Israeli army. 'Ben was normal, with a weakness and a strength,' she tells me. 'But when you are going on such a mission you need to be strong.' Describing a vivid memory of Ben, she says, 'Everyone connects in different ways and I remember his blue eyes. Always the way he looked, there was something … he had smiling, clear eyes.'

Rivka tells me she did not know that Ben became a Mossad spy. For months now she has voraciously followed media reports about Ben, some suggesting he actively betrayed his country, others saying that he simply couldn't handle the Mossad secrets he'd sworn to protect. 'He was not a traitor,' says Rivka. 'He was a victim, a victim of himself. He could not control himself.'

Rivka's son Yoni was close to Ben, having attended Bialik College with him during the almost four years the Vilands spent in Melbourne. They had been *shlichim*, or emissaries sent abroad and subsidised by the Israeli government to help foster youth movements. Yoni was one of the small group of friends who had known Ben was in prison before he died. So after visiting Rivka, I call him, hoping he will speak with me. Yoni is friendly on the telephone. As his job involves evening work coaching young tennis players, the only apparent difficulty in meeting him is finding a time when he will be free of work and family obligations. We agree to meet soon in a suburb of Tel Aviv.

On the morning of our meeting, I rush from my hotel, looking forward to an opportunity to flesh out my understanding of Ben's character. My phone rings as I am juggling the GPS in the hire car and attempting to deal with the unfamiliar sensation of driving on the right-hand side of the road. I am just ten minutes from his house, but Yoni is calling to cancel the interview. He is polite and says he understands why the book is being written. But like so many of Ben's friends, his willingness to talk has hit a significant brick wall in the form of Ben's family and that of his wife Haya. For nearly a year now, almost every time I have called or emailed one of Ben's friends, it has been reported back to his parents or his widow. This family is surrounded by a tight and resolute group of people. Each time the message is the same: no-one is talking to the media. Those friends of Ben's who had spoken to newspapers had been made to feel that they had done the wrong thing and had added to the family's burden.

Yoni cancels our meeting, expressing a sentiment I have heard repeatedly: he respects what I am doing, but he has given his word to the family. 'I'm sorry, Raffy, I can't do it,' Yoni tells me. I turn the car around and retreat through Tel Aviv's morning rush hour.

Days later, our paths almost cross when Yoni visits his mother at the kibbutz while I happen to be there. I don't actually see him because Rivka times my arrival to make sure her son is elsewhere on the kibbutz, celebrating a friend's birthday. Renewing our conversation, Rivka tells me that she only knew Ben properly when he was a boy. It was Yoni who was close to Ben in the last decade of his life, as he served his time in the army and later married. 'If the Mossad were to come to me and ask me about Ben, and at the same time they come to Yoni and ask him, they would get a different answer, because Yoni knows the man he was,' Rivka tells me. But I don't get to have such a conversation with Yoni. Akiva appears, and I get the feeling that Rivka wants to wrap up our meeting.

Akiva offers me a quick tour of the kibbutz, a polite way of telling me I am not expected to stay too long. As we walk around, I attempt to steer the conversation towards the subject of Ben Zygier, but it is as though I haven't spoken at all. Akiva treats my tentative queries as he would a fly that has just buzzed past his face, waving away the nuisance.

Akiva waves goodbye and watches as I steer my hire car away from the kibbutz. A few minutes later, I pull over to write down what Rivka said as she stood to farewell me in her spacious lounge room. It was only then that she'd finally hinted at how she really felt about Ben, at the double uncertainty that surrounds the life of a spy who couldn't confide in her and whom she can never ask what happened. 'Look, we didn't know Benjamin,' she'd said slowly. 'We had a picture. We saw him sometimes during these years and we love what we saw, but it was only a continuation of what we knew.' Acknowledging the fact that spies hide so much that they sometimes hide parts of themselves, she told me, 'The people who know him properly … know things that we don't.'

From Idealist to Activist

After returning from Machon, Ben began planning for a law degree at the Clayton campus of Monash University—like many of his contemporaries, he believed he could use the law to help change the world, and at the same time enjoy the prestige of the profession. Initially he remained passionate about Hashy, but as the months went by, he appeared to fit in less and less. He seemed unsure about whether he could continue to be a part of Hashy's particular ideology. He still planned to live in Israel, but the reality of the country's politics was changing and it was also changing Ben's point of view. Israeli society was becoming far more bitterly divided.

Hashy has a long history as a radical left-wing party that campaigns for social justice. In the 1970s in South Africa, it was shut down because of its agitation against apartheid. It was heavily involved in the socialist collectives called *kibbutzim* and it had been formally aligned with Israeli political parties that were staunch advocates of making concessions to the Palestinians and advancing the peace process. But the idea of consensus with the Palestinians was sorely tested by the 1993 Oslo Accords, which stemmed from secret negotiations in Norway's capital. The deal divided Israelis, and many Jews outside of Israel as well.

The rift in Israel was made wider by another event in 1993. The handshake on the White House lawn between Israeli Prime Minister Yitzhak Rabin and Palestine Liberation Organization chief Yasser Arafat symbolised peace for many, but Ben doubted the wisdom of that handshake. 'Yeah, he was ... a Likudnik,' says a friend, using the colloquialism for a supporter of the right-wing Likud Party, in which future prime minister Benjamin Netanyahu was a key figure. In his political thinking, Ben had only one ally, Dan Burrows, a fellow Hashy leader and someone he would remain friends with until his death. Both were on good terms with many in their cohort, but neither Ben nor Dan fitted in ideologically. 'They weren't really included in the end,' says someone who knew them both. 'They were pushed aside.'

But Ben was by no means an outsider in Hashy. 'People liked Ben,' says a friend. 'He was just a good guy. He was thought of as fairly intelligent. He was a fairly soft personality, not abrasive and not angry ... He had a kind of joker smile, with his eyes turned down at the corners. He was kind of normal, just pretty normal.' But the ideal of personally passing on the movement's ideology to the children around him was something that was becoming difficult for Ben. 'We had a lot of chats about it, trying to not change him but just show him the other side,' says a man who didn't agree with Ben's views but respected them. 'In the end, people like Ben are so determined … the guy wants to go to Israel and make a life, so good luck to him.'

As Ben carried out his law studies and Hashy duties through 1994 and 1995, Israel experienced an unprecedented wave of suicide bombings launched by the Palestinian group Hamas. The country's tabloids published graphic front pages of distorted bus chassis littered with the destroyed belongings of passengers, with sheets covering the remains of the victims. The attacks were a bloody backdrop to an increasingly bitter debate in Israel. Those on the right said the bombings were the inevitable result of Yitzhak Rabin's concessions.

Ben wanted to translate his opinions into actions. He wanted to help address what was happening in the Jewish homeland. He felt frustrated that Hashy just talked about the situation instead of doing something. So towards the end of 1995, Ben decided to take a break after his second year of university. He was going to do the one thing that was a constant in the collective experience of being an Israeli citizen: he was going to enlist in the Israeli army. At a time when Israeli society had never seemed so divided, Ben was going to join the very institution that was supposed to bind that society together.

Little did Ben know that as he went about finalising his plan, Israel's history was about to change dramatically and result in a terrible coincidence.

On 4 November 1995, there was a massive peace demonstration in the centre of Tel Aviv, in what was then called the Kings of Israel Square. Prime Minister Yitzhak Rabin stood on a podium in front of City Hall and looked out at more than 100,000 people. He condemned the Palestinian bombings but appealed to the Israeli people to have the courage to stick with him as he negotiated with Yasser Arafat. After thanking the representatives of countries like

Jordan and Morocco, who were a notable presence at the rally, he began his speech: 'Violence erodes the basis of Israeli democracy. It must be condemned and isolated.' As Rabin spoke, a radical Orthodox Jew called Yigal Amir moved through the crowd and positioned himself close to the steps of City Hall.

'This is not the way of the State of Israel,' continued Rabin. 'In a democracy there can be differences, but the final decision will be taken in democratic elections.' They were words meant for the substantial number of people from the Israeli right who were calling for the Oslo Accords to be dissolved. Hearing them, Amir would likely have been unmoved.

Rabin finished his speech and walked down the steps of City Hall towards the open door of his car. Amir raised his semi-automatic handgun and fired three times. Two bullets hit Rabin, one of them puncturing a lung, while the third bullet injured one of Rabin's bodyguards. As police seized Amir, Rabin was rushed to hospital where he died forty minutes later.

Polls consistently place Rabin at the top of lists of the 'greatest Israelis who've ever lived' and the 'most popular Israeli leaders'. Because Amir killed such an admired man, he holds a uniquely reviled place in modern Israeli history. 'Every murder is an abominable act, but the act before us is more abominable sevenfold,' said the judges who passed sentence on Amir in 1996. 'Not only has the accused not expressed regret or sorrow, but he also seeks to show that he is at peace with himself.' It is that lack of contrition that continues to shock Israelis. Nearly two decades later, Yigal Amir's brother and co-conspirator Hagai, who served sixteen years in prison for his part in the assassination, is also unrepentant. 'My brother had a lot more faith and determination to do it, even if it cost his life, something that at that time I was not yet ready for,' he said.[1]

Yigal Amir was given a life sentence, which was subject to the passing of a special law that ensures he will never be given parole. In 2003, Amir was taken to a cell specially built for him in Ayalon prison. It was designed so that he could be kept away from other prisoners, and guards could keep a close eye on him. Amir stayed in cell 15 for three years—the same cell that Ben would be imprisoned in for nearly ten months in 2010. The same security cameras that watched over Yigal Amir later filmed the last moments of Ben's life.

It was to be a dramatic and damning holding pen for Ben Zygier. He'd spent his life admiring Israel and had been fired by an ambition to join its elite ranks. It may have added to his despair and that of his family to be held in the same place as the man who'd done the unthinkable—slain a revered Israeli prime minister.

SOLDIER

Troubling Experiences

'In a place like Israel as you grow up, you know certain things are going to happen,' says a friend who knew Ben in primary school and grew up with him in Melbourne. This friend watched Ben try to face up to the challenges of learning to be an Israeli soldier, he saw Ben trying to deal with the pain of witnessing the deaths of army friends in an infamous helicopter crash, and he is not sure that Ben had the resilience that many in Israel seem to be born with. 'When you come out of cushy Melbourne, you're not exactly prepared,' he explains.

Even before his time in the army, Ben had experiences that shook him psychologically and left him susceptible to the later pain of solitary confinement. On his way between Melbourne and Israel at the end of 1995, Ben visited Egypt. While he was there he befriended a couple from Britain, with whom he formed a close bond. But before Ben left Egypt, the couple were killed in a car crash. Some people say he was devastated by the incident, that it was a hugely traumatic experience for him. No-one I speak to knows why Ben so quickly became so close to people he'd only just met, but whatever the circumstances, the loss was clearly something he never seemed to properly integrate into his life.

Ben began serving in the army in early 1996, soon after the incident in Egypt. He completed nearly two years of training as a regular soldier, and by all accounts, his experience of army life was a fairly routine one. He did, however, pick up a scar beneath one eye while on patrol in the Palestinian territories. He told friends he'd caught a rock in the face from Palestinian protesters. Other experiences were more troubling. Ben later told his friends he'd parachuted 'behind the front lines' and had been involved in skirmishes inside Lebanon. It's hard to know if such conversations from long ago simply took on a life of their own or whether Ben was the original source of the exaggeration, perhaps bragging and clouding the details of what he did.

Crash

At first Ben tried to get into one of the more selective paratrooper units, but he ended up in what was called the South Lebanon Liaison Unit, or Yakal. Since the 1980s, Israel had either had its own forces in Lebanon or it had supported proxies like the South Lebanese Army, usually made of up Christian Lebanese and Druze villagers who had a long association with Israeli forces. The unit Ben joined supported this proxy army, though most of the soldiers in it held administrative positions and were stationed inside Israel's borders. Israel and its proxy army controlled a small strip of territory inside southern Lebanon, on Israel's northern border. At least some in Ben's unit regularly ventured into Lebanese territory.

While he was a member of Yakal, Ben went through a horrific experience that left him psychologically fragile. 'He went a little bit nuts,' says one friend. It's a cruel term for a turning point in a complicated psychological history.

Ben told a number of his friends about his involvement in one of the worst air crashes in Israel's military history, which took place in the north of the country in February 1997. 'He told me there were two helicopters at one point ready for take-off,' says one friend. 'They were running for the choppers and one of them burst into flames and quite a lot of his mates died … and he just happened to be lucky enough to get to the other one.'

In reality, that's not what happened. Two Sikorsky transport helicopters carrying seventy-three soldiers were hovering in the air, waiting for official clearance to move off, when the rotor blade of one chopper hit the tail of the other and both came crashing down. There were no survivors. Ironically, the soldiers were going to be taken by air into Lebanon to avoid the risk of travelling on roads that were sometimes mined by Hezbollah. The accident had a remarkably high death toll considering the fact that fewer than seventy Israeli soldiers had died in Lebanon in the preceding three years, mainly while fighting Hezbollah. The crash not only prompted national despair but also sparked debate about whether Israel should pull out of southern Lebanon. There was an official day of mourning during which cafes and movie theatres were closed, and media broadcasts were dominated by a rollcall of the names of the dead and interviews with their friends and families.

Ben was profoundly affected by the accident, says a friend who was in Israel at the time. The incident almost certainly hastened his exit from the army, which took place at the end of 1997. But later, there would be little acknowledgement that Ben had any mental health issues when he ended his military service. The official line after Ben's death became public was that he had left the Israeli army fit and healthy.

Tzvika Levy heads the Lone Soldier Project, which helps distressed soldiers who have no immediate family in Israel. 'Towards the end of his service [Ben] became frustrated and awaited his release,' Levy told *Ha'aretz*, adding that Ben 'had some health problems, including stress fractures'.[1] But Ben was clearly suffering from more than stress fractures. He even spent some time at

Kibbutz Gazit trying to recover his equilibrium. Finally, he made the decision to return to Melbourne to finish his law degree, rationalising that it was better to get his professional qualification in Victoria than to start an undergraduate degree from scratch in Israel.

Some of Ben's Israeli friends saw this as equivocation, a degree of hesitation about his commitment to his new country. But that wasn't the issue. His legal career notwithstanding, Ben seems to have been trying to deal with the trauma of what happened while he was in the army. In Australia, he saw a psychologist about his army experiences. He mostly kept his suffering well hidden from the people who were closest to him, but he did sometimes open up about his difficulties. 'He certainly gave me the impression that he was upset about things he had seen in the service,' recounts one of his friends. Even four or five years later, while he was working as a lawyer in Melbourne, Ben was still referring to the chopper accident. 'He seemed to be emotionally still affected by it,' his boss at a Melbourne law firm tells me. 'We were always wondering why on earth anyone who had grown up in Melbourne would go and do something so dangerous.'

A Standout Guy

The queue to get into the Prince Hotel in the late 1990s was often raucous and long. It was one of the more popular nightspots in Melbourne, a key feature of the bustling revival of the St Kilda precinct. On reaching the front of the queue, some young Jews were surprised to find Ben Zygier working as a doorman. He was employed at the Prince on the weekend while he was studying law. Ben scrutinised his peers as well as his friends, so it was a job that required more than confidence—it necessitated equanimity in the face of drunk, drugged and sometimes angry people.

'It's not like a war zone but there was a lot of pressure,' says the man who gave Ben the job, Israeli-born Dror Erez. Erez had a prior connection to Ben, having briefly been in a band with Deborah

Conway and Willy Zygier. As part of the then management of the live music venue, Erez was happy to have Ben marshalling the unruly crowd. 'He was a standout guy, he was ex-army,' Erez tells me. 'I think Ben was a terrific guy with an amazing ability to communicate to people. To be a doorman so young, you can understand, that's not a common thing because normally people don't have the maturity to deal with that.'

It seems that on Ben's return to Melbourne, his inner demons didn't have an impact on his outward self-confidence. In private he could be fragile. Publicly, he was simply an ardent Zionist who was happy to be back in Australia, living with his parents, for the time being, but who would soon return to Israel.

Ben's confidence was also noticed by those he studied with at university. 'He was an ex-soldier. He wasn't a big guy but you know, he had this thing about him,' says one university friend. Many who knew him speak of his ease with strangers and his affability—if he wanted to speak with you, that is. When I ask Ben's friends whether they were surprised to learn that he ended up working for the Mossad, many say 'No' without much hesitation, such was his confidence and desire to prove himself.

Completing his undergraduate law degree took Ben three years and led to a position in a commercial law firm called Deacons. From the twenty-fifth floor of the Commonwealth Bank building in Melbourne's CBD, Ben could watch thousands of daytime shoppers streaming in and out of Bourke Street Mall. He still nurtured a dream to live in Israel. He visited Israel often to catch up with his friends, refresh his sense of patriotism and stay connected with the country, and he would proudly display photos of a trip when he returned. He wanted to establish his credentials as a lawyer in Victoria before moving back to Israel. And so he spent two years travelling into the city every day, to the mid-tier law firm where he was gaining experience in the world of mergers and acquisitions.

'You know, I'd have to say, he was a good friend during the time that he was there,' says Christian, who was Ben's supervising partner for much of the time he was at Deacons. 'We would go and have a drink after work. He was really likeable, and I am completely amazed with what I have since found out.' Even lawyers admit that while large law firms are often full of intelligent people, the work itself and the professional environment can be dull. And commercial law firms don't always attract the most diverse recruits. But Ben clearly stood out. He intrigued people, even those who were five or ten years older than him. 'I was just interested in him. He was a dynamic person,' says Christian.

Ben spent his first year at Deacons doing his articles, in effect serving his apprenticeship as a lawyer—working for relatively low pay to earn his certification. Christian wanted Ben on his team when those who'd been accredited were allocated permanent positions. 'We got a choice, and he was one [junior lawyer] that we were happy to have,' says Christian. Many young lawyers who've just finished their articles don't want to stand out too much for their personality. They often just put their heads down and trust that what will be noticed is their hard work. But Christian tells me that Ben was not like that: 'He was very clever. But one thing that he had was a level of charisma which was above average … He had more self-confidence than almost anybody else at his level.'

Like so many who worked or studied with Ben, Christian didn't know until the news of Ben's death broke in 2013 that he had been employed as an Israeli spy. The media coverage portrayed Ben as someone whose damaged ego led him to freelance as a putative spymaster, a man doomed to fall into an enemy's trap and divulge secret information. Christian read the reports avidly but couldn't reconcile them with the person he knew as a lawyer in the early 2000s. 'He seems to be portrayed as a pretty narcissistic, self-interested, arrogant person,' Christian ruefully assesses, '[but] I must say I didn't get that impression at all. I thought he was intelligent and fundamentally very likeable.'

I ask Christian whether he'd had any doubts about trusting Ben with commercially confidential information, and he gives a lawyerly answer that perhaps reflects his new-found doubts: 'I never had the impression that he had breached that confidence.' But when I ask whether Ben could have inadvertently divulged secrets, Christian is far more passionate and unequivocal. 'When I heard about this I was completely shocked, and I was quite upset about it, because it just didn't seem like the person I knew,' he says.

When I ask Christian for specific memories of Ben, his sense of humour is instantly recalled, as has happened when others have answered the same question. Christian tells me how he once travelled to London for work and had to hook into a large conference call with Ben in Melbourne and others in offices around the world. 'One of the other solicitors was rabbiting on for about fifteen minutes and it was getting terribly boring,' remembers Christian. 'Next thing I knew, I get an SMS message from Ben! He is on the other side of the world, basically making a cheeky comment about how this is just going nowhere.' To Christian, this was part of Ben's appealing character: 'He was cheeky. He was a funny, likeable character, and he had a good sense of humour.'

Ben's passion for Israel was also obvious. Christian says, 'He was pretty patriotic and said he had been involved in very dangerous operations, what he sort of said were behind-the-lines missions.' Christian was another one of those who heard firsthand the story about the helicopter crash.

After five years in Australia, for reasons that are not entirely clear—perhaps work-related, perhaps impulse—Ben decided to once more act on his passion. Christian says that one day Ben came into his office and resigned: 'He was going to go over there [Israel] and work on contracts with some big law firm in Tel Aviv.' On the surface, the change of country was a bigger deal than the change of jobs. But it was at his next law firm that Ben would set foot on a path that would lead to Israel's overseas spy service, and a job that would lead to his death and his public excoriation.

RECRUIT

The Approach

At the base of a Tel Aviv office block, workers rush out of franchise bakeries carrying plastic-capped coffee cups and takeaway lunches; they flow past the gleaming windows of anodyne restaurants. Above them stretches the building that houses Israel's biggest and most prestigious law firm: Herzog, Fox & Ne'eman. This is the prime place in Israel for a commercial lawyer with overseas experience. It's ideal for a new immigrant who is keen to demonstrate their legal credentials and excel in Israel's small but high-pressure business world.

It was to this firm that Ben relocated at the start of 2003. Just like his time at Deacons, Ben was put to work in a large team handling contracts for significant commercial clients. It was another notch in Ben's belt, a sign of achievement at a visibly high level. A friend of Ben's tells me that while it was not something he wanted to boast about, he did feel the need to be an 'achiever of great things'.

It was when he was working as a lawyer in Tel Aviv that Ben was first approached about a career with the Mossad. The intelligence agency has a small network of 'spotters' who look out for potential recruits. Sometimes these spotters, or *sayanim*, are former Mossad employees, sometimes they're people who have provided advice to the agency or performed small, non-clandestine tasks that required no legal breaches. One of these *sayanim* worked as a partner at Herzog, Fox & Ne'eman and asked Ben if he'd be interested in talking about some 'interesting work'.

This is not how Ben's entry into the Mossad has been reported. In my shabby hotel room in Tel Aviv, I reread reports in the German magazine *Der Spiegel* and Australia's Fairfax newspapers that claim Ben approached the Mossad, not the other way around. The reports say that he used a Gmail account to make contact via the Mossad website and then sent in a fax to outline his involvement in a Zionist youth movement, his time on a kibbutz and details of his army service. However, multiple sources I've communicated with in Australia and Israel have insisted that the first contact between Ben and the Mossad occurred when he was approached by a partner at the Israeli law firm where he worked. It is possible that this partner asked Ben to apply to the agency and oversaw the filling in of forms. It is the first of many significant discrepancies between what has been reported about Ben and what I am told in Australia and Israel.

Ben was not the first youth movement graduate to be approached by the Mossad. Until the early 1980s, almost two-thirds of the people who went to Machon later lived in Israel—though by the time Ben started his army service in the mid-1990s, the flow of Machon graduates who then lived permanently in Israel had been reduced to a trickle. And when someone from that small Machon subset made that decision, it was not unusual for him or her to receive a phone call, a letter or a tap on the shoulder.

In Israel, I ask people who graduated from the Machon whether they were approached. The typical response is relaxed, but it surprises me. 'Oh yes, most of us got the call,' says a man who keeps in contact with many of the Anglo immigrants who have been to

Machon in the past few decades. 'They approached so many of us, especially the Australians.' Youth movements are not designed to feed recruits into Israeli intelligence, but they are an attractive reservoir of potential employees for the Mossad.

To many of those who knew Ben, it was obvious that he didn't want to live in Israel as just another immigrant. Ben was driven, interested in testing himself to satisfy his own curiosity about his abilities. His Hebrew was almost flawless, he spent twice as much time in the army than he needed to, and he deliberately sought out a competitive career. And when it came to the Mossad, he saw a chance to become part of one of the most revered institutions in the country.

An Organisation of Warriors

Israel's spy agency has a domestic reputation that can only be dreamed of by the US Central Intelligence Agency, or CIA, and Australia's intelligence organisations. Responsible as it is for the collection of overseas intelligence and for covert operations, the Mossad is venerated by most Israelis as an organisation of warriors battling the country's enemies, striking out at them before they can attack.

Professor Mordechai Kremnitzer has worked as a military lawyer and prosecutor, an adviser to various Israeli cabinets and as the head of Israel's Press Council. His simple assessment of the Mossad is that Israelis 'need it, we depend on it and therefore we trust it'. Professor Kremnitzer also sums up why Ben's story is so alluring to the Israeli media: 'Someone who is a Zionist, who loves Israel, who at the same time was suspected to be a traitor … this is very dramatic, this combination of contradictions in one person.'

The Mossad has always been keen to attract Westerners. This is because Westerners do not act and talk like native-born Israelis and so they don't need to be trained to forget their identity—they have a ready-made second nationality they can use as a genuine disguise. In its early years, the Mossad recruited from a pool of Jews born in Arab countries whose parents had come to Israel since 1948 and could pass as locals. During the 1970s, the escalation of conflicts between Israel and its neighbours coincided with the greatly increased ease of jet travel. Western recruits could now more convincingly pose as tourists or business travellers.

In the 1990s, Canadians, New Zealanders and Australians became especially attractive recruitment targets. Their countries' neutrality in the Arab–Israeli conflict meant their accents and some-times genuine passports provided easy access to the nations Israel most needed to penetrate: Syria, Lebanon and Iran. 'It's not unusual that *olim* [immigrants] work for [the] Mossad,' confirms a man who was approached by the agency. 'But what happened to [Ben], it's unbelievable.' During my visit to Kibbutz Gazit, Rivka Viland tells me, 'One like Ben, he wants to be a good one, one of the best … And once you are part of a special unit, the Mossad, you start to come under pressure, strong pressure.'

In search of others who may have been approached for recruit-ment by the Mossad, I seek out someone I grew up with, whom I'll call 'David'. He'd been a few years ahead of me in Netzer and he'd gone to Machon and made *aliyah*. I knew him and his two broth-ers reasonably well; I'd laughed and sung with them. But when I try to contact David through a good friend of his in Melbourne, the response my intermediary receives by text is gentle but firm: 'If Raffy calls asking for his mobile number, don't give it to him.'

Chancing my luck on the internet, I do a Google search and David immediately turns up as a Mossad employee, a detail revealed in a WikiLeaks file. In one entry, he is described by the US embassy in Tel Aviv as a senior intelligence official working in a national security job focused on finance. He is also cited talking about ways Israel can control the funds going into the Palestinian territories, and how to work with the United States on economic sanctions against Iran. He was, of course, unaware at the time that all this would later be made public via Bradley Manning and Julian Assange.

This revelation was a shock to me. It sent me scurrying to the dusty cupboards in my parents' home in Melbourne to dig up old photo albums. I soon found a picture of me and a group of friends, a smiling David among us. Taken in 1988, it showed a bunch of high school kids dressed in daggy clothes and staring intently into the camera at the end of a Netzer winter camp. We had stayed somewhere cold in regional Victoria, in a conference centre or something similar, preparing ourselves for a year away in Israel. David had been my *madrich*, playing the same role for me that I had played in looking after and educating Ben. I remember this man telling us not to believe the 'propaganda' that portrayed Israeli soldiers as the aggressors in the first Palestinian intifada in 1988. He helped prepare me for Machon and encouraged me to spend the year after high school in Israel. Now he is apparently working out how to control the international aid money going to the Palestinians and has a high-security clearance with Israeli intelligence.

I have been very close to several other people in the photo. One of them recently made the commitment to go and live in Israel. He was one of my best friends for most of my teenage years. Another boy is now a man I'm proud to call one of my closest friends. I met him at Netzer when I was about twelve and he continues to influence my life. He tried living on a kibbutz for a while in the 1990s, but he returned to Australia and now lives just outside Melbourne. One of the girls in the photo remains a good friend too. She also gave life on a kibbutz a try and settled in Israel for a while with another good friend of mine. But they decided against a permanent stay.

Many non-Jewish people have said to me that they don't understand why Ben left Australia, where he grew up, to live in Israel. For me and my friends it was a matter-of-fact, everyday occurrence for people we knew to shift halfway round the world—not for a job opportunity or to live in a cultural centre like New York or London, but to join a uniquely Jewish nation. It is the very purpose of the ideology that is disseminated inside Jewish youth movements. The truth is that I could well have done what Ben did; I could have joined the Israeli army. Many of the people I knew could have enlisted and gone on to join the Mossad. Researching Ben's story has made me realise that while I wasn't particularly close to Ben, his world and mine often overlapped.

I start flipping rapidly through my photo albums and turn up another picture. It shows me grinning into the camera while perched on a green hilltop somewhere in Galilee. My hair is blowing in the wind and I've jauntily plunged one hand into a pocket of my shorts. I'm wearing a Midnight Oil T-shirt that makes a mockery of the American flag, the stripes replaced by a blue barcode ready for scanning at a supermarket checkout, and dozens of miniature hands substituted for the stars. Nestled in the crook of an arm is an AR-15 assault rifle, pointed arrogantly at the sky. A group of us from Machon had just been on a day-long hike, and whoever had been our security guard had let me pose with his weapon. It was the sort of photo I'd long craved to have taken, simply because boys older than me had returned to Australia from Israel with similar pictures.

The allure of military involvement was strong in those middle months of my Israel adventure in 1989. A few weeks after the hike, we were taken to the country's military cemetery in Jerusalem. It was Israel's annual Day of Remembrance, which commemorates the deaths of all the soldiers who have been killed in war, as well as the victims of bombings. There are so many names that it takes most of the day for them to be read out on national TV. We were being educated about Israel's history so we could be part of its future. I remember with gut-wrenching certainty the promise I made to myself as I sat by a gravesite. I was going to join Israel's army to protect the Jewish nation. I had no other choice.

The feeling eventually faded—in hindsight, I don't think my promise felt genuine for more than a few weeks. But I spoke about it for years afterwards, and I educated other children before sending them on their year-long trips to Israel, encouraging them to consider a similar future.

Nothing Revealed

Sharon was one of the many who attended Machon and later made the move to Israel. In 1999, a few years after settling in the country, she received a cryptic letter from the Prime Minister's office.

'It said if you're looking for interesting work overseas, please call the number below,' she tells me. The letter was subtle, deliberately secretive. 'At first I thought this is so ambiguous that it doesn't sound serious at all,' Sharon explains. 'It was like one of those ridiculous ads you see in the paper: "If you want to earn really good money, you should call!"' Because of the official-looking letterhead and the individual code number, Sharon thought it was likely a letter from the Mossad, or perhaps the domestic spy service, the Shin Bet. 'I'd heard of this kind of thing before, that they try to recruit immigrants who are ideological, but I'd kind of never thought about it,' she says.

Sharon had made the move from Melbourne because she loved the State of Israel. She still does, despite all the flaws she sees, and the development of a more pragmatic view of the country as she has matured. And for every *oleh*, or Jew who chooses Israel as their home, the experience of being chosen by one of the state's elite institutions always evokes some pride. 'I also felt a bit chosen, like I must have something worthwhile to give to this country,' Sharon tells me. So she called the number on the letter to ask precisely who wanted to recruit her. 'I wanted to know even though I knew they wouldn't tell me,' Sharon reflects. 'I was curious also about the work involved.' But she did not get very far. 'They ignored my question,' she says. 'It was a woman who said, "Are you interested?" And I very quickly understood that they weren't going to reveal anything and the ball was in my court to decide if I wanted to proceed.'

Some of Sharon's friends said she should go along and see what was being offered. But she decided to seek the advice of her father, who has lived in Melbourne for decades but was born and raised in Israel. When she called him, he took a deep breath and fired back: 'I've never interfered with your decision-making before, but I'm asking you, and telling you, not to work there. You won't have a life.'

Each year for three years, just after her birthday, Sharon received the same letter of invitation. After the third message, Sharon tried a different tack. She called the number provided on behalf of a friend of hers who did want to work for the Mossad. She also told the letter sender: 'Get off my case completely! I'm the wrong profile for you, I can't keep a secret. Please just don't bother with me anymore!'

A few years later, Sharon was still seeking a definitive answer about precisely what job had been on offer. She met someone who worked for the Mossad and handed over the three letters for verification. Yes, she was told, the letters were from the Mossad. Sharon expected the letters to be returned, but her acquaintance destroyed them, which upset her—she'd wanted to show them to her children, and eventually to her grandchildren.

Whenever Sharon has recalled the offer in the years since it was first made, her father's advice has rung in her ears. She says he'd been inadvertently prophetic, given what happened to Ben Zygier: 'He told me that he did some work for them, and once they don't need you they toss you away like rubbish.'

Another Good Choice

The evidence suggests that at the end of 2003, after having spent a year with Herzog, Fox & Ne'eman in Tel Aviv, Ben was accepted for training by the Mossad. I ask a former colleague of Ben's whether he was an obvious recruit for an intelligence agency. 'No, not at all,' the man says. 'Just his persona … [his] stature, I mean you're talking about a guy who was 5 foot 8 at best and just didn't look that way inclined.'

Most of us have learned what we know about spies from popular culture, and it is an axiom of espionage that even the most mundane details of intelligence agencies are kept hidden. This secrecy warps much of our understanding of the type of people these agencies seek out—especially if, as in other spheres of professional life, these organisations employ a wide array of people. Ben's former colleague admits it is simply too difficult to know how well suited Ben would have been for this type of work: 'He was physically capable without being strong or overly robust or overly fit, and he didn't project any of those sorts of skills. But then … who knows what happens in intelligence agencies?'

Over the past twenty years, the Mossad has had to work hard to attract new recruits. For decades after the creation of the State of Israel, the inherent social prestige that went with being a fighter pilot, army commando or Mossad spy was almost unquestioned. But by the 2000s that had changed, with young Israelis—like youth in other countries—having become more sceptical of authority, more aware of the myriad options they could pursue, and less willing to commit to the strictures of institutions such as the armed forces and intelligence agencies. What made recruitment even more difficult was a series of high-profile Mossad mistakes. The aborted assassination of a senior Hamas official in Jordan in 1996 and the arrests of four Mossad agents who were tapping phones in Switzerland in 1998 occurred at a time when many Israelis were beginning to question the worth of their high-profile institutions and their politicians. So the Mossad recently has had to fight ever more entrenched apathy and has laboured to show recruits what it can offer, and not just to potential spies—the Mossad also needs drivers, mechanics, clerical staff, foreign language teachers, IT professionals, chemists, laboratory workers, technical designers, clinical psychiatrists, electricians, audiovisual technicians, carpenters and lawyers, among others.

The Mossad has no public affairs office, not even a direct number to call. Its website and social media activities, such as on Facebook and Twitter, offer the only windows into the agency's modern-day recruitment efforts. The agency's current chief, Tamir Pardo, writes on its website that he wants 'only the finest and most suitable people'. This is accompanied by the equivalent of an advertising slogan: 'The Mossad is open. Not to everyone. Not to many. Maybe to you.' But the site does offer more than bland slogans. It describes the character of the people the Mossad wants, which perhaps reflects how the agency sees itself: 'If you have boldness, wisdom and intelligence, you could have an influence and make a national and personal achievement.' One line seems particularly well suited to someone like Ben Zygier: 'If you can provoke and motivate people, then you are likely to be made of the raw material that we are looking for.' Ben had always been willing to probe someone else's views, and he had spent years at Hashomer Hatzair motivating young people to form a closer relationship with Israel.

Over the years, the Mossad has welcomed many people with the desired characteristics. And in 2003, it thought it had made another good choice, a lawyer called Ben Zygier.

SPY

The Basic Skills

Throughout 2004, Ben would have received an intense induction followed by a unique education in the skills he'd need if he were to succeed in the highly desired operational section of the Mossad, called Caesarea. First there is a raft of screening tests that Mossad recruits have to endure, many of them psychological. There is also an initial one-on-one interview with a psychiatrist followed by a panel interview with other mental health experts and experienced Mossad officers. The impact on Ben of the deaths of his fellow soldiers in the 1997 helicopter tragedy doesn't seem to have handicapped him in these tests, as he made it through his induction. But ever since Ben's case became public, this induction process has come under intense public and parliamentary scrutiny. According to the Mossad's Human Resources Department, it is now more rigorous.

Ben was taught how to follow people unobtrusively and detect if he was under surveillance himself. He was also taught simple forgery skills and the art of adjusting documents, as well as how to crack open email accounts and copy and transmit computer files undetected. When it came to modern information flows, Ben knew what he was doing. A man who spent time with Ben during and after his work in Europe for the Mossad, someone who knew him well, tells me he was 'technically competent. He was good with computers. Always, in terms of the internet, he just really knew his way around.' To the Mossad, such proficiency may be a basic skill required by its operatives, or it may be a focus of the training that some agents, like Ben, have received.

Ben was also taught how to work at one job while unobtrusively focusing on another. Working undercover is at the core of what it means to be a spy. This requires a commitment to quiet discipline, a willingness to memorise plans for any contingency and an appetite for humdrum routine. Mossad recruits are taught the importance of patiently and diligently performing a conspicuous task while quietly acquiring what outwardly seems like unimportant information. Such discipline allows someone like Ben to work in a seemingly innocuous job while being a small but significant contributor to a larger flow of information. Much of this work is not glamorous, and it can be boring, but it is essential.

Lying for a Living

Spies like Ben are trained in how to deceive, how to misdirect people's attention, how to lie. Ben sometimes needed to deceive his friends, and mostly he could not talk to them or his family about what he did. Those closest to him learned not to ask how he occupied himself, and contented themselves with the knowledge that he would tell them what he needed to, or when he could.

Ben used details of his own life to create easy-to-remember and convincing cover stories. He sometimes told people he was 'working for the army' and went on to describe a place that bore many similarities to Israel's massive defence ministry headquarters, which was adorned with a distinctive tower and just happened to be located next door to the law firm of Herzog, Fox & Ne'eman. It was a useful and easy way to manage deception when only a few of his closest friends knew he worked for the Mossad.

Most people involved in espionage need to lie. It is what they're taught to do. But few who've had the training talk about it openly. 'I have to lie a lot' is the frank admission of a senior Australian security employee who has agreed to talk with me. He checks that the cafe where we meet is unobtrusive and casually glances at anyone who walks past our table more than once. He acknowledges that every spy agency faces a potential problem in training people to lie: getting them to stop. When an agent, an officer or a source is used to telling people outright falsehoods every day, there is a danger that this lack of honesty can bleed into their personal lives. As a result, conversations with colleagues, superiors and other agencies can be contaminated. 'It's one of the biggest issues we face,' the man tells me.

This is precisely why the vetting for intelligence agency jobs is so rigorous. The Australian security man says that often, those who remain after all the physical and psychological testing are not an elite force of hyperintelligent, super-fit overachievers. They're more likely to be regular, dependable men and women who are some-times a little dour and not always noticed at first as standouts by their colleagues.

John Kiriakou, a former CIA case officer who played a part in the capture of a significant al-Qaeda leader in 2002, made a more overt declaration: 'People are trained to lie for a living. They lie to everybody. They lie to convince people … [that they] are their best friends, to the point where targets are willing to commit treason.' Another former US security agent labelled Kiriakou's views ridicu-lous and melodramatic, but in a frank interview on US television, Kiriakou maintained there was a standard approach to training intel-ligence agents around the world. 'One part of lying is convincing others to do something they otherwise might never do, to persuade them to comply with a simple request that they would normally ignore,' he said.

While speaking to those who knew Ben, I am told, unprompted, about just such a request that he made. During his training, Ben was still socialising with his friends in Israel, happy to chat when people bumped into him in the street in Tel Aviv. The consensus among his friends is that at this time he was his usual, affable self. But two people remember a specific request he made of them—he asked if he could borrow their Australian passports for a short time. Neither person remembers the precise reason Ben gave, but the request itself stuck in their memories because they both thought it odd and refused to comply. When news of Ben's death broke many years later, it is something they told their friends about—subsequently, I received independent confirmation of what had taken place.

Such a request could have been part of Ben's training, to see if he was able to persuade his friends to do something they normally would not do. Or it could simply have been Ben practising his skills of persuasion, seeing how far he could go in getting other people to listen to him. Or these requests could have been a genuine Mossad effort to have a good look at the sorts of passports that might be available for their operations. Regardless, his blunt appeal and talk of passports presaged some crucial events in his life.

In mid-2004, while Ben was undergoing his training, two Mossad agents on the other side of the world got caught out. Their botched mission in New Zealand also swept up Australia in its slipstream. It was a rare public glimpse of how the Mossad worked, demonstrating just how far the organisation would go to obtain a single genuine identity that its spies could use. The incident also may have laid the seeds for Canberra's retaliation against Ben Zygier a few years later.

Kiwi Conspiracy

In November 2003, three Israeli citizens arrived in Auckland within two days of each other. Thirty-year-old Uriel Kelman had two passports, one Israeli and the other Canadian—four years earlier, he'd picked up a new Canadian passport from the country's embassy in Auckland to replace one he said had been lost. Another visitor was fifty-year-old Eli Cara, an Israeli citizen who'd been living in Australia and had travelled between Sydney and New Zealand for his travel agency business twenty-five times since 1999. The third arrival was Zev Barkan, who'd travelled on a US passport. All three were Mossad agents who were in the country to try to harvest New Zealand passports.

Barkan soon identified a potential target, a wheelchair-bound man who lived in residential care. Because of his cerebral palsy, this New Zealander had never left the country and so had never applied for a passport. Barkan obtained a copy of the man's birth certificate. Using the target's name, he then visited an Auckland GP, citing a minor ailment, and at the end of the consultation casually asked the doctor to witness a passport application. 'He was calm and gave me no reason not to believe him,' the GP later told a NZ court. 'So I filled out the form.' To avoid detection, the Mossad agents set up a post office box and voicemail service for the passport application.

This ruse might have gone undetected, but one member of the passport office staff decided to make some additional enquiries about the application Barkan had made. When he telephoned Barkan, he was surprised to hear that the man had a strong North American accent—this from an applicant who supposedly had never travelled overseas. According to court documents, the passport officer testified: 'When I quizzed him on his accent, his explanation to me was he had not travelled or held a New Zealand passport before, but he had spent a lot of time in New Zealand with Canadian friends and family.' It was probably the best excuse Barkan could come up with on the spot, but it was dubious enough to kick off an investigation by New Zealand Police. When they contacted the father of the profoundly disabled man, he was surprised to hear about his son's new passport. But police let the application proceed because they wanted to see who would accept the new document.

The Israelis did not want to personally receive the passport, so they arranged for an elaborate series of deliveries. They'd provided the address of a local company on the application form but asked for the passport to be sent by courier to a second address, an apartment elsewhere in Auckland. As the courier arrived, Cara was watching from a nearby cafe. He'd telephoned the manager of the apartment block and arranged for the passport to be delivered by taxi to a third address. A police summary for New Zealand's District Court explains what happened next: 'As the taxi driver got out of his vehicle and approached the apartment entrance, the defendant Cara got up from his position at the cafe and directly shadowed the taxi driver into the apartments.' The Mossad agent had been trained to know when he was under surveillance, but this time his training failed him. Cara was quietly arrested and a police officer left with the taxi driver for the passport's final destination. Kelman was waiting and watching at the third address, but something alarmed the more experienced agent and he quickly walked off, even trying to hide his mobile phone in some nearby bushes. But the police grabbed him. The final member of the trio, Barkan, had already left the country.

As New Zealand's foreign minister at the time, Phil Goff had been worried that passports might be illegally obtained and used for espionage. He tells me over the phone from Auckland, 'Effectively what we had was a criminal act … using those identities obviously for the purposes of [the] Mossad, people using those sorts of passports to commit assassinations and other very serious acts.' Goff says it marked the lowest point of New Zealand's relationship with Israel: 'We don't expect that from our friends, and we've always regarded Israel as being a friendly country.' Goff continues: 'Israel wanted us to drop the charges, to sweep it under the carpet, and we said, "No, we won't interfere in the process of justice."' Israel would not confirm that the two arrested men were Mossad agents. And according to the police summary, Cara and Kelman gave no explanation for why they wanted the New Zealand passport; they even claimed they didn't know each other. New Zealand's then Prime Minister, Helen Clark, was outraged, stating that the men could be charged as spies. She was reported as saying, 'We have very strong grounds to believe these are Israeli intelligence agents.'

At the time of his arrest in March 2004, Cara was an active, mid-level operative within the Mossad's Caesarea section, the same department that Ben Zygier would join. Kelman's Sydney-based travel agency supposedly catered to Israelis travelling the world after their compulsory military service, but his real business was as a Mossad project manager for a passport factory.[1] (A subsequent internal examination by the New Zealand Government found that a number of Kiwi passports had previously been forged or procured by the Mossad, and these were cancelled or red-flagged.) Kelman had an odd cover story for someone posing as a travel agent in Sydney. Not long before his arrest, he told some people he'd befriended that he would soon be travelling, 'something to do with West European embassies'. One man told the court that Kelman 'never told me specifics about the company he worked for, but it was something to do with security and detecting bugs'.

'I don't know why other countries think when they come to New Zealand that we're operating in a Third World manner,' Phil Goff tells me. I ask him if he was surprised the Mossad agents were caught. Goff pauses, then says, 'You'd think that they might have worked harder at it.'

New Zealand's response to the scandal was angry and forceful. The 'strongest diplomatic retaliation in twenty years, since French spies bombed the *Rainbow Warrior* in 1985' was the classified observation by Auckland-based US diplomats, contained in cables published by WikiLeaks. One cable said Helen Clark went beyond the recommendation of her foreign policy advisers, imposing a six-month freeze on relations with Israel. 'We don't want to be seen as a soft touch by any other country that thinks, "OK, we can do this in New Zealand and get away with it,"' Goff tells me. 'Being a small country, actually we are more likely than not to detect that.' In the wake of jail sentences of a few months for Kelman and Cara, Tel Aviv and Auckland mended relations. But the New Zealand response is a yardstick for measuring the possible reactions of other countries should the Mossad misuse their passports.

The scandal had an Australian connection. While the two Israeli men were in prison in Auckland, they were visited by a mid-level official from Israel's embassy in Canberra. His name was Amir Laty, and he had also observed their trial. Just months later, in December 2004, Laty was expelled from Australia on the advice of the country's domestic spy agency, the Australian Security Intelligence Organisation, ASIO.

There had been speculation about Laty's relationships with several women while he was in Australia, including the daughter of Liberal MP Philip Ruddock, who was the federal attorney-general at the time and so had direct ministerial responsibility for ASIO. Laty left the country just before he was able to accept an invitation to Christmas lunch with Ruddock and his family. There was no suggestion of anything other than a platonic friendship between Laty and Ruddock's daughter. Ruddock explicitly denied Laty's departure was related to his daughter, and Kevin Rudd, who was the Opposition's foreign affairs spokesman at the time, would only say that Laty had been expelled over a 'national security matter'.

Some in the Jewish community in Australia, however, have suggested that Amir Laty was expelled in an example of tit-for-tat diplomacy because Cara, who was based in Sydney, had been trying to get Australian passports. This has not been verified, but there almost certainly would have been conversations at the time between ASIO and the Mossad as a result of the New Zealand fiasco, which may have led to significant tension between Australia and Israel.

In a notable coincidence, around the same time Laty was expelled from Australia, Ben Zygier made a brief trip back to Melbourne. He was in Australia because he'd just been given his first mission working undercover for the Mossad. Using the first of three Australian passports, he applied at the Italian consulate for a visa to work in Milan.

The Spymaster

Understanding who ran the Mossad during Ben's time there is crucial to understanding the organisation's reaction to what Ben did and why he was so severely punished. From the time of Ben's recruitment into the Mossad in late 2003 through to the time of his death, the intelligence agency was ruled by one of its best-known, most revered chiefs, Meir Dagan. Short and squat, his stature matched by his rough and gruff nature, Dagan was charged with transforming the Mossad and focusing Israel's espionage efforts on Iran. He oversaw Ben's missions from 2005 to 2008, and the following year was told of concerns about Ben's loose talk. The diligent collection of information that Ben had been trained for was a key part of the quiet revolution inside the Mossad, even as it renewed its reputation for very public assassinations.

Meir Dagan was born in 1945 on the floor of a train as his mother was being deported from the Soviet Union to a Nazi camp in Poland—Dagan's personal roots in the last great existential threat to the Jewish people help explain his focus as Mossad chief. Dagan speaks in small, clipped sentences and has the brusque nature of a man with rough beginnings. Central to the public mystique that surrounds this ruthless hunter of Israel's enemies is a photograph of his grandfather. The picture used to hang on the wall of Dagan's office at the Mossad's headquarters, north of Tel Aviv. It shows Dagan's grandfather on the day he was killed in 1942 in the Polish town of Lukow. The man is kneeling, and in a gesture that combines fear and defiance, he has his arms raised over his head with clenched fists and his prayer shawl draped around his shoulders. One Nazi soldier is looking directly at Dagan's grandfather, his rifle slung over his soldier. Another soldier is looking happily at the camera, a truncheon in his hand. 'Look at this picture,' Dagan reportedly urged visitors to his office. 'This man, kneeling down before the Nazis, was my grandfather just before he was murdered. I look at this picture every day and promise that the Holocaust will never happen again.'

It was in 2002, when Israel's outspoken Prime Minister Ariel Sharon was looking for a new man to refresh and reorganise the country's overseas spy agency, that Dagan was recruited. Sharon, who had been close to Dagan in the military and knew well his fearsome reputation, told the Mossad's new head to restore the agency as a fighting force, as an institution that is prepared to carry 'a dagger between its teeth'. Sharon wanted an agency that would target and kill its enemies, something it had become much less adept at doing in recent times. He wanted someone in charge who would shake up the Mossad and reverse its reputation for being too timid, not daring enough, not willing enough to venture into enemy territory. Meir Dagan fit the bill. He is said to have begun each weekly meeting at the Mossad with the phrase, 'So, who are we going to assassinate today?'[2]

When I am in Israel, I try to contact Meir Dagan, but I can't persuade anyone to hand over his mobile phone number, so I settle for emailing his assistant. The reply reads: 'Thank u for your mail but Mr. Dagan is not available this week.' I later send another email asking if I can discuss Dagan's meeting with Geoff and Louise Zygier after Ben's death—I have been told this meeting took place, but I haven't been able to verify it. This time there is no reply to my email. These refusals are polite, which is at odds with Dagan's public reputation.

In the early 1970s, Dagan developed a record as a merciless commando leader in the Gaza Strip. Under his general, Ariel Sharon, Dagan led an army unit that disguised themselves as Palestinian labourers and taxi drivers in order to track down and kill militants. It was an Egyptian newspaper that first reported on the ruthless Israeli army leader who apparently chopped off the heads of his enemies— Sharon confirmed this when, as prime minister, he said Dagan's special skill was 'separating Arabs' heads from their bodies'. Dagan took this trademark brutality to the Mossad, which under his leadership is thought to have carried out more assassinations in more hostile countries than it ever had before. And the man's reputation seems to have some grounding in reality. One soldier told an Israeli newspaper that Dagan would 'wake up in the morning, leave his room, take a piss with one hand and shoot at soda cans with the other'.

Dagan was responsible for a new perception of the spy agency as having tentacles that reached everywhere. As well as being able to smite its enemies deep inside their own territory, the Mossad developed sophisticated systems to watch over, understand and sabotage its targets. The agency's chief took on many of these tasks personally.

Meir Dagan also took control of a multifaceted effort aimed at just one country: Iran. It was important to keep tabs on Lebanon and Syria, but Tehran's nuclear program was the priority. Israel had nuclear weapons and it was—and still is—determined to maintain its strategic advantage. So Dagan pushed for international travel bans on Iran's nuclear scientists, urged sanctions against various Iranian companies and travelled to Arab capitals to explain such measures. Importantly, under Dagan, the Mossad tried to find out about every piece of business Iran did outside its borders. That meant tracking shipments of seemingly innocent items, such as tiny screws and electronic components, as well as the computer programs and industrial machinery that could be used for producing missiles. The Mossad gathered as much information as it could about electronics, communications and industrial processes, even the patterns for the special steel needed to construct the centrifuges that concentrate uranium. It wanted to know about anything that could be part of Iran's nuclear effort, as well as that nation's broader military and intelligence capabilities.

There are many WikiLeaks-released cables that demonstrate how diplomats from various countries told their US counterparts that Meir Dagan was the go-to source on Iranian industry and its business links abroad. The work that was done by Ben and his colleagues at a small company in Italy was one of the many streams of information that fed into Dagan's wider view of Iran.

From Milan to Iran

When Ben went to the Italian consulate in Melbourne to get his visa at the start of 2005, he would have presented his Australian identity. There would have been absolutely no mention of his Israeli citizenship and his impeccable Hebrew, and certainly not his new position inside the Caesarea department of the Mossad. Ben must have been excited as he began his first mission for Israel's elite espionage agency. Less than three years after living at his parent's home in Malvern and working as a Melbourne lawyer, Ben was going to be a spy living in Milan. But while he may not have realised it, he was still just a small cog inside a big machine.

The Italian company Ben was placed with had its office near the centre of Milan and a bigger technical facility in one of the city's industrial suburbs. Operating across the Middle East and Africa, the firm provided satellite capacity for everything from pay-TV transmission to ship-based communications, and had hundreds of employees. But its size was not as important as its clients—this company did business in Tehran. As far as I can tell, Ben didn't understand the details of satellites and their communications, and so could not provide technical assistance to clients. But he was in a position where he could see what services those clients required, what they were using and where they were being used. Significantly, he was able to travel to Iran.

In the write-up of a joint investigation with *Der Spiegel*, Fairfax journalists Ronen Bergman and Jason Koutsoukis contended that Ben never travelled to Iran on company business. They were assured of this by the man who ran the company Ben worked for. That man also told the journalists that Ben had no face-to-face dealings with clients. However, sources tell me that Ben did travel to Iran on more than one occasion in 2005–06. I am also told that he travelled there with another Australian, a more senior employee of the Milan-based company. This Australian man was a Mossad agent too and travelled to Iran even more often than Ben did.

It is difficult to know precisely what Ben and this other Australian man were doing in Iran, but I am told Ben had the more junior role, probably that of obtaining information. The other man may have recruited informants, penetrated more companies and per-haps looked for other places to obtain data. These are all complex tasks. Even those agents who recruit informants can have separate responsibilities. One group of agents may simply support the others in doing the recruitment. Another set of agents may focus on tracking potential contacts, physically or electronically, or monitoring those already providing information to the Mossad. A third tier of agents may meet with and identify potential recruits, sometimes those who are compromised in some way—sometimes it is left to another agent to finally recruit a source.

What we do know is that within the Italian company, Ben was promoted rapidly and was soon communicating directly with Iranian clients. The firm's CEO described Ben to Koutsoukis as 'extremely sharp' and said the Australian was usually the fastest of his employees: 'By 11 in the morning, he had finished tasks that would have taken others the entire day.'[3] The CEO then said that while Ben had a role in keeping the company's accounts, 'it was soon clear to us that he had no experience in this area', but he 'was so talented that he soon acquired the necessary skills'.

The company head also told Koutsoukis he could not see how the Mossad could have gained any advantage by placing agents in his company. But this is disingenuous at best. It's unlikely a company would admit that Ben had access to important information. Protecting its business relationship with Iran would be a high priority for the firm, and it clearly would not want to publicise its work with Tehran. Also, Ben was not simply a bookkeeper in accounts. Satellite services provide clients with crucial links to the rest of world, which is why the Mossad spent a number of years using multiple agents to try to penetrate communications companies doing work in Iran. We do not know how successful they were, but it's reasonable to assume that even if only small details of such an operation were exposed, it could endanger agents and sources. And, potentially, millions of dollars might be wasted if those activities were shut down prematurely.

Ben's initially successful tenure at the Italian company soured after eighteen months and the Mossad dispatched him elsewhere in Europe. 'We had to let him go in late 2006,' said the company's CEO, telling Koutsoukis this was because Ben lacked motivation.

But there was another factor. Just before his departure, Ben had a dispute with a client over the payment of a bill and threatened to cut off the client's services. His boss was horrified—it could have left possibly hundreds of thousands of people without pay-TV services and severely embarrassed the company. Ben may have seen this as a legitimate negotiating tactic, but it may also have been an early sign of a lack of stability. If so, this doesn't appear to have been recognised by the Mossad.

A Quick Coffee

I'm sitting by a new waterfront development in Tel Aviv, in a cafe that overlooks a massive wooden walkway designed to evoke the industrial life of the seaside docks that were once at the heart of this city's working life. Crowds must pack the place on a weekend or public holiday, but today it is comfortably busy. The couple sitting next to me do not notice as an Apache attack helicopter flies south, parallel with the sand—only in Israel do the machines of the military mix so innocuously with the modern shopping experience. I am thinking about what other work Ben might have done in Europe. And as I am unable to speak to Meir Dagan about this, I consider trying one of his predecessors, Ephraim Halevy.

In contrast to Dagan, Halevy speaks like the consummate diplomat that he is. Born in England, he is the urbane nephew of the Cambridge philosopher Isaiah Berlin. Halevy was brought in to lead the Mossad in 1998, soon after a bungled assassination bid in Amman. The personal envoy of five different Israeli prime ministers, he has even nurtured a public profile, having been interviewed on US television programs like *The Daily Show*, hosted by the comedian-turned-commentator Jon Stewart.

I finally convince myself to cold-call the former Mossad director on his personal mobile phone. Sipping a double espresso, I dial Halevy's number—it feels like a minor success of my trip to Israel to even have phone numbers like this to call. When Halevy answers, I begin to explain that I've come to Israel to do some research, but he gently interrupts to say, 'Welcome to Israel!' I tell him that I am examining the changing nature of the personalities of those recruited as spies around the world. It is a ploy. I've decided not to mention Ben Zygier by name but to keep my request vague, to give myself a greater chance of success. Who am I kidding? I'm not sure if it's simply because I am from Australia or if it's because this man has had more cryptic conversations in a month than I've had in my career, but the ploy fails. Halevy acknowledges my interest but says it would not be long before the conversation would turn to recent events. Although it's inevitable that this conversation is about to end, I ask whether it might be possible for us to meet, just for 'a quick coffee'. Halevy's response is smooth and at the same time quietly disturbing. He says that not for a coffee, 'not even for a double espresso', would he meet me, because the subject matter would drift into areas that he is not interested in approaching.

The mention of a double espresso jolts me, as it is what I always order when I meet up with people in Israel. I try to work out how he knows what I drink, then I just ask him, with a smile on my face. But he does not reply. That's when I check myself, aware that I'm back in that hall of mirrors again, surrounded by reflections of my own limited understanding.

Paranoia is a professional hazard when reporting on those who work with classified information. In Australia, people I've met with have asked me to turn off my phone, even to take out its battery, to minimise the chances of surveillance. Some sources have quickly stopped talking when lone men have walked past our table, while others have written down rather than spoken names and other details out of fear they might be overheard. You never know whether such precautions are the result of pure nerves or practical common sense. Still, sitting in this waterfront cafe, I have trouble convincing myself that any intelligence agency is interested enough in this book to bother watching or listening to me, let alone recording what I drink.

When Ephraim Halevy finally farewells me, he says, with gusto, 'Enjoy your stay in Israel!'

Shared Experiences

When I stepped off the plane at Tel Aviv's Ben Gurion Airport to do some research for this book, it was my first visit to Israel for seven years. As I passed through a glass-encased walkway that looked over a massive circular shopping plaza in the middle of the terminal, a familiar feeling welled up unbidden within me. It was a feeling planted when I was a young child at Netzer, and it still runs deep. I can only try to convey it in words: 'All these people are Jewish. Everywhere I go in this country, the vast majority will be Jewish.' Spread across the gilded space of the terminal, which was filled with cafes, gift shops and electronic billboards displaying departures to places as far-flung as Moscow and Dakar, were people who shared in this glorious mosaic of cultural and tribal experiences. Many of them would have had the same Jewish cultural cues inculcated in them. They'd recognise the family dynamics and shared experiences that mean two people from very different countries end up having a lot in common. As I looked out over the large concourse, bordered by towering pieces of sandstone etched with biblical characters, I remembered that to many people, being Jewish can be a deeply cultural, deeply internal experience, far more passionate and binding than the vague strands of identity they experience in countries like Australia or Britain.

This powerful idea was also reflexively at the forefront of my mind when I scanned the streets of Tel Aviv and Jerusalem. The unifying idea of a Jewish nation still resonated strongly with me. Precisely what it means to be Jewish, how it can be defined, who can be included and who cannot—these are questions often confined to universities and cafes, sometimes to synagogues and even the parliament. But the concept of a Jewish nation is unquestioningly accepted by the majority of those who make it up. Ben had come to have this same experience, and he was devoted to his new country. It was a devotion he would share with the woman whom I have called 'Haya'.

As he dealt with the initial flush of excitement of his first year abroad working for the Mossad, Ben was also getting closer and closer to his girlfriend. In some intriguing ways, her background mirrored Ben's. Her parents were Australian, and decades before Ben had, they'd made the ideological decision to leave the country of their birth to go and live in Israel. As a result, Haya seemed to have a relaxed Australian nature, without being flippant, yet she also had the passion of a native-born Israeli, without an urge for overt displays of emotion. She was also smart, resolute and had a steely will.

Most importantly, Haya understood what it was like for someone to haul up their roots and go and live in an entirely different culture. This was likely soothing for Ben. The fierce ideology of a youth movement cannot totally prepare a new immigrant for the drastic transition of an international move. Many people who travel from Western countries to Israel end up taking extended breaks in their countries of origin because the relocation can be tough. For the average boy from the Australian suburbs, the challenges of living in another country, serving in a foreign army and joining a spy service would be daunting.

While it has been reported that Ben was asked to leave the company in Milan, I am told that Ben's marriage to Haya in the Israeli summer of 2006 was a key reason for his departure. The short-term stints of work he then embarked on in companies around Europe enabled him to get back to his wife in Israel more often.

Stuxnet

The Mossad believed that Iran and Syria had set up 'front' companies to help move money and weapons around the world, and it was determined to identify them. Ben was part of this effort to block the front companies and also to interfere with the genuine ones—to find out 'a little bit more about what's going on in Iran and Syria', a source tells me. Much of Ben's work was painstaking, methodical and dull, but I'm told it was also considerably successful. He and agents like him gained good knowledge of business links inside Iran. This intelligence was constantly being added to the already comprehensive picture that the Mossad had developed, providing an ever-clearer view of Iran's industrial and military network.

One Australian security source assures me that Ben and his colleagues were part of a significant Mossad operation that targeted Iran, explaining that 'they built themselves a platform that required considerable planning, expenditure … it was a very important asset for Israel's national security, and ultimately for the benefit of the West'. I can't determine which broader successes or failures flowed from Ben's particular operations, but to understand the general importance of his work, you only need consider two devastating attacks launched on Tehran's nuclear program. The first, the sharp end of the Mossad's focus on Iran and its most public and blood-thirsty work, was the assassination of Iranian scientists and military leaders. The other, done in partnership with the United States, was the remarkable sabotaging of Iran's nuclear equipment using a computer virus.

Iran's nuclear research facilities, in the town of Natanz and at the Bushehr nuclear power plant, had previously been briefly derailed. The power supply, which came in from Turkey, had been disrupted, and Israel and the United States had also warped the vacuum pumps that were imported as a vital component in uranium enrichment.[4] These efforts had capped off the gathering of a wide array of industrial, commercial and communications data by spies and informants, and through intercepted calls and emails. But ultimately, this meddling merely resulted in Iran stepping up the physical security around its nuclear program, as well as electronically insulating it from the rest of the world—the scheme was disconnected from the internet, supposedly sealed off from cyberattack.

So, again with the help of the United States, Israel planned a new type of assault. Former US intelligence chief Michael Hayden referred to it as 'the first attack of a major nature in which a cyber-attack was used to effect physical destruction'. He was talking about a computer virus codenamed 'Olympic Games'. It was, said Hayden, 'an attack on critical infrastructure. Somebody has crossed the Rubicon.'[5]

Buried deep underground within Iran's nuclear facilities was the machinery used to concentrate uranium for the warhead of a missile. Thousands of tall, silver-coloured centrifuges spun furiously to purify the raw material needed for an atomic weapon. Inside each centrifuge were delicate rotors. If these rotors didn't spin at precisely the right speed, they could destroy the centrifuges, or at least nullify the effort to concentrate the fissile material. Controlling this process were small 'programmable logic controllers' or minicomputers. It was these minicomputers that were specifically targeted by the 'Olympic Games' virus.

The minicomputers had been designed by the German company Siemens and operated a simple software program that ran on Microsoft Windows. The Israel–US virus was engineered to promiscuously spread via Windows. The virus would remain benign until it hit the right industrial system—it would only attack a Siemens system, and it would only target machines that spun at certain speeds, which included some of the vacuum pumps as well as the enrichment centrifuges. The worm also had a built-in self-destruct mechanism to destroy the computer code that carried it, making it very hard to trace.

Much of the technical work on the virus was done by Israel's Unit 8200, which is similar to the surveillance-focused National Security Agency in the United States in that it maintains much of Israel's electronic spy network, monitoring conversations and communications. The project is thought to have utilised the largest malware team ever assembled, and it's also believed to be the most costly computer sabotage ever carried out. To ensure the virus would have the intended effect, the United States reportedly purchased its own industrial centrifuges, infected them with the virus and then watched as the machines broke into pieces. These busted components were later displayed in front of President George W Bush in his office, as proof of the program's potential.[6]

While the United States and Israel shared the credit for creating this sophisticated piece of computer malware, only the Mossad had the knowledge and ability to physically get the worm into Iran's nuclear facilities. The delivery of this electronic weapon was only possible because of the Mossad's comprehensive understanding of Iran's industrial landscape, such as knowledge of which pieces of machinery had been bought for ordinary industrial purposes and which had been deployed in the nuclear program. The work done by agents like Ben made this understanding possible. There was surveillance of Iranian scientists, including their families, friends and daily routines, and monitoring of the technicians from Siemens who were helping the scientists in Iran to fine-tune their equipment.

What the malware needed was an unwitting carrier. An unknown number of USB sticks were loaded up with the virus and distributed through the Mossad's network in Iran. Eventually, the virus was carried past the Iranian electronic and physical security barriers at the nuclear facilities. The haphazard use of the USB sticks also meant that the virus was carried back out, at which point it was sophisticated enough to report back to its controllers on the effectiveness of the sabotage. However, after leaking out of Iran's nuclear facilities, the virus began to spread and eventually infected millions of computers around the world. It had become more virulent than its designers had possibly intended, somehow activating itself beyond the realm of the Siemen's minicomputers that were meant to be its sole target. Soon there were copies of the worm all over the world and analysts gave them a collective name— Stuxnet, after key words in the virus's coding.

It was a fiendishly clever piece of malware that did not arouse suspicion in Iran's nuclear program for months, perhaps even years. Sometimes it caused the uranium enrichment to fail, while at other times it prompted various parts of the centrifuges to explode. Not only did it slow down and speed up the centrifuges, it also hid these changes from the computers that monitored the machines, so sometimes the Iranians shut down entire stands of centrifuges in an attempt to understand what had happened. One of the worm's designers was reported as saying, 'The thinking was that the Iranians would blame bad parts, or bad engineering, or just incompetence.'

Israel has never confirmed it was behind the virus, but its officials have broken into wide smiles when asked about it in media briefings. And at the retirement of a very senior army officer, a celebratory video of his achievements included a reference to the worm.

Killer Instincts

Israel also took the more direct approach of targeting Tehran's nuclear program by killing the people who were crucial to its success. The peak of the assassination program in Iran occurred between 2007 and 2011, the headline result of work done by agents like Ben. It was this sort of dramatic violence that helped create the public mystique that continues to draw people like Ben to the Mossad.

In Iran, Israel perfected a particular type of attack that could have come straight out of a James Bond film. A nuclear scientist's car would be followed through morning rush-hour traffic by one or two people on a motorbike. The bike would move up alongside the car and one of the riders would lean over and attach a magnetic explosive device—a so-called 'sticky bomb'—to the door nearest the person he was trying to kill. Seconds after the motorbike sped off, the bomb would detonate, triggered either by a timer or by remote control. The bombs were small but powerful, and the casings were shaped so that the explosion targeted the person closest to it. In some of the bombings, the people who were sitting next to, in front of or behind the target emerged from the blast with just cuts and bruises.

These attacks sent shock waves through the small scientific community relied upon by the government in Tehran, and they also spread fear abroad. Iranian scientists, high-ranking Syrian officials and Hamas commanders—they all spent considerable time and money ramping up their own security in the wake of the killings.

The Mossad was also blamed for a spectacular explosion at an Iranian missile base. Most of the seventeen people killed in the blast were from Iran's elite Revolutionary Guard, including Major General Hassan Moghaddam, who was regarded as the architect of the country's missile program. The base had also housed some Shahab-3 missiles, the likely vehicles for Tehran's nuclear warheads if they were built.

Not all of the Mossad's assassination attempts were successful. In November 2010, just before Meir Dagan's retirement as head of the agency, one of the biggest prizes of all got away. The head of Iran's atomic energy organisation, Fereydoon Abbasi-Davani, was well trained or simply lucky when he and his wife got out of their car just moments before the vehicle blew up. Some reports suggested that he recognised a clicking sound on the door of his car and quickly urged his wife to jump out. His colleague Majid Shahriari was not so fortunate—on the same day and at roughly the same time, Shahriari was killed in Tehran by another motorcycle assassin.

These assassinations were a signature achievement of Meir Dagan, and by the time he left the Mossad his agents had become well practised at hitting targets outside of the Iranian regime as well. In Lebanon, they killed Hezbollah's military commander, the clever but murderous Imad Mughniyeh, who had been impli-cated in multiple bombings of American bases and the kidnapping of high-profile Westerners in Lebanon in the 1980s; he was also wanted over bombings in the Jewish community in Argentina in the 1990s. Mughniyeh had been spotted on the Israeli–Lebanese border in 2000, but the then Israeli Prime Minister, Ehud Barak, had decided against an assassination in a territory that his coun-try had just withdrawn from. With Meir Dagan as the Mossad's chief, however, killings in other nations were no longer avoided as extreme options.

On a calm evening in Damascus in 2008, Israeli agents watched as Mughniyeh left a reception at the Iranian embassy. When the Hezbollah commander walked past a Mitsubishi Pajero, the agents detonated a remote-controlled bomb inside the car, completely destroying it and also ripping Mughniyeh's body to pieces, although the blast did little damage to the surrounding buildings. The Mossad had clearly known Mughniyeh's movements—where he usually went, where he felt most comfortable. To gain this knowledge, the organisation probably coordinated dozens of agents and informers in Syria for months, if not years, ahead of the hit.

Also in 2008, Israel targeted Syria's general Muhammad Suleiman, who played a role in his country's nascent nuclear program. Again, the victim was killed in a place where he thought he could relax and be safe, at his beach house just north of the country's historic crusader forts at Tartous. It is generally accepted that Suleiman, a close ally of Syrian president Bashar al-Assad, was shot to death. But reports differ as to whether he was sitting in his car, wading off the beach or sitting on the balcony of his house when he was gunned down, and whether the shots came from a sleek yacht or from an Israeli naval vessel moored offshore.

We may never know how Ben's work fitted into this wider tapestry. Meir Dagan's efforts, on the other hand, are easier to quantify. Israel's targeting of Tehran has been estimated to have delayed Iran's nuclear ambitions by anything from five to seven years. But despite what appears to be a well-deserved reputation as a planner of daring and dangerous missions, Dagan's legacy has been oversimplified. When he was declared 'Man of the Year' in 2008 by one Israeli TV station, a newspaper columnist derided the choice: 'Our man of the year is a declared killer, whether by box-cutter or car bomb. His craft is killing and his killer instincts are our source of pride, the peak of our creativity.'

It's impossible to know whether the Mossad is actually responsible for every death attributed to it, but after his retirement, Dagan clearly felt wearied by the emphasis on assassinations when much of the Mossad's work is more subtle, and perhaps more effective. In an interview on Israeli television in 2012, he went so far as to reject his bloodthirsty reputation: 'It's bullshit—there is no joy in taking lives. Anyone who enjoys it is a psychopath.'

SUSPECT

Raanana

In mid-2007, two and a half years into his operational career with the Mossad, Ben returned to Israel to work in Tel Aviv. He moved out of the more active Caesarea department and into the bigger, more bureaucratic part of the Mossad called Tsomet. This meant he was desk-bound and faced work that was more analytical and potentially less exciting than his duties overseas. I am not able to establish whether Ben saw this as a demotion, or whether it was intended as such by the Mossad or was simply part of the normal career progression within the agency. Regardless, it was reported that this development was frustrating for Ben, a blow to his aspirations.

In Ben's personal life, however, important things were happening with Haya. For the first time in the couple's married life, Ben was based in Tel Aviv. They'd set themselves up in the northern district of Raanana, one of the city's better commuter suburbs.

As I drive into this neat, manicured suburb, I try to imagine what Ben and Haya's life was like here. I move slowly down a street elegantly lined with blossoming jacaranda trees, aware that this is one of those rare places in Israel where the streets are uniformly clean and most of the buildings look refreshingly contemporary. Very few areas in the country have that home-on-a-block look that comforts so many Australians in their suburban houses.

I can't find the couple's apartment, perhaps because I have been given the incorrect address. Even if I did find it, I'd be a little wary of approaching it. Adding to the layers of secrecy blanketing Ben's life, a court order has been in effect at least since his death, forbidding any Israeli journalist from even approaching Haya. It's unclear whether such a law also applies to me, or how heavy the penalty would be if I breached it. But it is enough to make me doubt the wisdom of pursuing Haya's address too closely.

In the centre of Raanana I spot a park that Ben and Haya's friends have told me was a key part of their life. It is a gorgeous lawn-filled reserve, with a sprawling playground, climbing equipment and a huge area for playing sports and riding bikes. The park has an almost amphitheatre-like quality. On this weekend afternoon, birthday balloons have been tied to an outer fence to denote the prearranged spot for a children's party. Kids practise their rollerblading and chase each other on scooters, and anxious toddlers call to their parents. The only thing that doesn't fit with this suburban idyll is the sentry with a handgun holstered to his hip who sits at the gated entry to the park. But most Israelis don't notice such security because it is a familiar sight—they pay it about as much attention as the colour of a shopping mall.

I'm told that Ben settled back in Tel Aviv mainly because of the impending birth of his first child, 'Naomi', who arrived in November 2007. By this stage, after long aspiring to serve, Ben had already experienced Israel's army and the Mossad. Once Naomi was born, Ben may have felt he would never again achieve such elite, front-line roles, though he also may have felt ambivalent about this. 'Around your twenties is an extremely crazy time [in] many people's lives, and people change tremendously,' says one friend of Ben's, alluding to the particular combination of confidence and frustration that seemed to mark Ben's life.

Under Pressure

Tracing the changes that were happening in Ben's life at this time is difficult. But sometime after the end of his work in Europe and subsequent settlement in Raanana, he went through a crisis. The memory of the deaths of his fellow soldiers a decade earlier, the pressure of a life of espionage and the strain of taking care of a child all likely took their toll. The Mossad had made a 'big mistake', Ben's friend Lior Brand told an Israeli newspaper in March 2013. 'There's very painful mistakes around it. They took the wrong guy. He couldn't deal with it.' Brand, who had served in the Israeli Air Force, said, 'Ben was not cut out for pressure like that. Most people are not cut out for this kind of stuff. I wasn't cut out for it.'[1]

Brand was not the only friend who felt that Ben was not well equipped for the significant changes that came with his recruitment and deployment by Israel's intelligence agency. Another person who was close to Ben says, 'A guy like him, getting away from home, living in different countries, living a secret life, I mean who knows the sort of changes that can occur.' And like many who associated with Ben, this person is confused by what they don't know about his final years.

Those who knew Ben were always trying to work out what he did with his time. One friend tells me this 'was something that came up quite a bit' in conversations with him. The vague answers he gave about his work, behaviour and frequent overseas trips only fuelled the speculation. Members of his extended family would even ask his friends, 'Do you think he works for the Mossad?' Some knew he did and couldn't admit this. But others believed this couldn't be true— they figured that maybe he worked for the army, in intelligence, but that there was no way he worked for the Mossad.

The pressure Ben was under led him to make several suicide attempts. From what I'm told, one was in early 2008, possibly in

Israel, and involved him 'walking out into traffic', according to one friend. It has also been hinted to me that Ben attempted to take his own life the following year. It's difficult to confirm exactly what happened. Some friends assure me that these attempts at self-harm occurred before he joined the Mossad. Who knew about the attempted suicides and what help Ben received are some of the most closely guarded details of Ben's life. One trusted source tells me that by the time Ben was in prison, his wife and parents knew about these incidents. But surprisingly, judging by the court documents, it seems that the Mossad and the prison service did not.

It's my understanding that Ben did not tell his employer what had happened, but that general personal issues were a key reason why he was granted special dispensation to return to study in Australia. In mid-2008, he applied for an Australian Government–funded loan to help pay for a postgraduate management degree (similar to an MBA) in Melbourne the following year. Perhaps the Mossad was beginning to acknowledge what Lior Brand would point out years later: that Ben 'was in over his head. They put the wrong guy in the wrong situation.'

Contradictions

Perhaps it is unsurprising that at this time of great psychological pressure, Ben appears to have made a big mistake. What I discover about Ben's alleged error, however, differs significantly from what has been previously reported in *Der Spiegel* and the Fairfax news-papers *The Age* and *The Sydney Morning Herald*. The Fairfax stories, written in 2013, staked their credibility on references to the many friends and family that journalists Jason Koutsoukis and Ronen Bergman spoke to, as well as references to meeting Mossad sources, one of whom was inside a limousine with darkened windows. Regardless, I disagree with some of the central allegations—my own investigations lead me to different explanations.

Bergman and Koutsoukis said that Ben was disappointed to be given the desk job in Tsomet, that he was frustrated at being rotated through another part of the organisation and was desperate to prove he could do more in the field. They reported that Ben was crushed by the move back to Tel Aviv and felt that he was perceived by his colleagues as having failed in Europe—he was 'neither particularly bad nor particularly good, but mediocre', according to one of their sources. But no-one I speak to mentions this frustration.

The reporters' central allegation is that in 2008, Ben decided to prove his worth by securing a trophy, and that without telling anyone at the Mossad, he flew to Eastern Europe. On this trip, Ben reportedly established contact with an associate of Israel's Lebanese enemy Hezbollah, in order to groom them as a double agent. But he was allegedly outsmarted while trying to prove his Mossad credentials, and he ended up passing on classified information that exposed two of Israel's own double agents in Lebanon. The *Der Spiegel* and Fairfax stories asserted that these Israeli sources were arrested and jailed by the Lebanese authorities. They also claimed that this chain of events was revealed by Ben under interrogation by the domestic intelligence agency Shin Bet in 2010, that in fact he made many damaging and shocking admissions.

One thing that concerns me about this allegation is that the two Israeli double agents turned out to have been arrested with dozens of others on charges of spying for Israel. It is possible that, even in the midst of such a massive security sweep, those two arrests were the result of Ben's betrayal. But when I ask for the views of other journalists in Israel and Australia who've reported on security and intelligence for many years, none of them believe the story. Small details seem to have been left out, including the fact that one of the more high-profile Lebanese double agents had already been let out of jail.

This concern doesn't mean much on its own, but it does make me suspicious that perhaps the Mossad was happy to plant doubts in the media about Ben's abilities, to suggest that Ben was explicitly responsible for his own downfall. Crucially, these stories drew attention away from whatever Ben had known about Iran.

The Koutsoukis–Bergman story has clear implications: Ben's motives were good, but he was incompetent and, most importantly, he'd done something outrageous, utterly beyond the bounds of what was acceptable. This perspective seemed to explain his suicide. It also implied that Ben lacked the fundamental skills needed for front-line intelligence work. The problem for me isn't that some of these elements might not be true, but that the story is so neatly tailored to serve the Mossad's interests.

Koutsoukis tells me that he and Bergman were essentially told that Ben was a fabulist, an exaggerator willing to act on his own illusions. 'And that was a big weakness, a big personal character flaw,' he says. 'I don't know if [the] Mossad knew or realised. I had been told that when he [Ben] was in Melbourne, he was talking up his experiences in the IDF [Israel Defense Forces], [saying] that he had been involved in some battles and that he had been injured … But that was an exaggeration. He hadn't been involved in any of the battles, but he had been shot at.' Koutsoukis is right about the exaggeration, but I believe he is wrong about the central allegation concerning the trip to Eastern Europe.

Later, my doubts are made concrete. A source in Tel Aviv tells me that the story published by Koutsoukis and Bergman was simply wrong. I am surprised, but then an Australian Government source gives me the same assurance. My informants insist that none of this supposed freelancing by Ben in Eastern Europe ever occurred, and that the decision to return to Tel Aviv in 2007 was driven by Ben's desire to live with his wife and prepare for their first child. They dispute that Ben would ever have made an unauthorised trip such as the alleged visit to Eastern Europe, and they also say he never met with anyone associated with Hezbollah.

This complete contradiction of what has been previously published about Ben presents me with a dilemma. Just as the Fairfax journalists cannot tell me precisely who they spoke with, my sources have credentials that I cannot discuss without betraying their trust. Their credibility can only be demonstrated by divulging specific pieces of information, but these I cannot share in this book. I can only say that the details I received could only have come from inside the security services in Israel and Australia.

I also have to weigh up what I have been told by Ben's family, friends and workmates, and the people who watched what happened from the sidelines. These comments have had to be tested against what I already knew and what other journalists have already published. One of the toughest questions for me to answer is whether Ben would have acted as reported by Koutsoukis and Bergman. Even among those close to him, recollections vary. Some of Ben's friends accuse him of arrogance, though none accuse him of making things up. 'He wasn't a stupid person. He wouldn't just blabber about without control,' says someone who saw him frequently in 2009. Another friend agrees, telling me that Ben 'was a pretty quiet sort of shy guy, most of the time, and all the stories that say that he told everyone that he was working for [the] Mossad, I mean he didn't tell me'.

However, Ben clearly angered some of those he was closest to. 'He had this macho thing going on. He was sometimes really up himself,' one good friend tells me. The speculation about Ben's work helped feed an impression of inconsistency, if not hubris. 'He was a bit unstable,' continues the friend, 'hot and cold, like today he is your best friend then he doesn't speak to you for a week.'

There's a consensus that Ben was very good at talking to strangers, especially those with whom he wanted to establish a connection. One friend says he always 'did well talking to women', another that he 'was very good with women'. But others saw his talkative nature as a sign of too much confidence. 'He was very arrogant,' says one female friend. 'He had more female friends than male friends. He pissed a lot of guys off.' Quite a few people also say that they often didn't know what to expect from him. 'No, not arrogant and macho, just very hot and cold,' says a long-time friend. 'If he was your friend, he was great fun to be around. But one morning I called him and woke him up and he just cracked the shits and for me that was it … But then later he came back and he was fun again and he'd just call randomly, just talk to you and swap funny jokes.'

Ben is not described as someone who betrayed confidences or lied about his exploits, not by any of the people I speak to who knew him in the last years of his life. One friend says that while Ben was a bragger, given to exaggeration, he was not someone who made things up. Yet that is precisely the image that appears to have been embraced by many of the journalists who reconstructed his life after his death. 'Arrogance is the wrong word,' says a former law firm colleague of Ben's. 'There was a great deal of self-confidence and a very buoyant character, but to hear or to read some of the stories now, [it] is all a bit of a surprise. There must be more to it because his character was not that way inclined.' Another man who knew him well says, 'He was not a big-shot army guy, he was always just a bit quiet. When he opened up he was funny and he could be a little bit loud, but that wasn't his personality.'

However, much of my research agrees with the suggestion in many of the published stories that Ben's boasting was the ultimate cause of his downfall. I am never told that he went as far as flying unauthorised to another country to conduct freelance espionage. That event I am explicitly told did not happen. But Ben's willingness to mouth off was a problem. No-one suggested Ben did this maliciously, or that his talkativeness came from a desire to further his own Mossad career. Ben got into trouble simply because he just didn't know when to shut up.

I ask a friend who had known Ben since the late 1990s whether he was a bragger, and the reply contains an interesting observation. 'I just think that he had the potential to be a blabbermouth,' the friend says. Explaining himself, he refers to Ben's ability to communicate. He says that Ben's belief that he could speak with anyone, that he could persuade anyone, could have led him to expose secrets. 'I'm not saying that he did,' the friend tells me, 'but he was such a lovely guy, he was so confident with his words, so confident of himself. And if he ended up being "the bunny", it wouldn't be the first time in the history of espionage. It's not inconceivable.'

Ben's friend has looked me in the eye for much of our conversation, but now he pauses, looks down at the ground, then delivers a final judgement: 'It's a bit like being a great pilot but making a mistake one day and crashing.'

Mood Swings

Ben and Haya's lives back in Melbourne in 2009 were packed with the stresses and pleasures of a young family. The Caulfield apartment where they lived with their daughter was big, light and airy. One of four apartments within a 1960s building, it is more like a medium-sized house than a flat, with parquetry floors, white walls and a modern but not quite contemporary kitchen. The three bedrooms were filled with the usual detritus of everyday life. 'There were millions of toys everywhere,' says one family friend. His paternal grandparents had lived in the flat for several decades, and a young Ben and his sister had attended Friday night dinners there to celebrate the Jewish Sabbath. Ben's grandfather had sat at the head of the table and his grandmother at the other end, so she could be close to the kitchen.

The street on which the building sits looks like any other in this pocket of Caulfield, a combination of apartments, newly built architect-designed homes and older Federation and Art Deco bungalows. It's only a brief drive to St Kilda Beach, while a short stroll away are synagogues and kosher delis that grow in number as you near Balaclava, the most distinctly Jewish area in the city. The streets nearby are replete with ultra-Orthodox Jewish men wearing fur hats and odd-looking black, seventeenth-century European suits.

His neighbours describe Ben as always helpful, and happy to stop and chat. The elderly woman who lived beneath him, and who has been in the block for nearly fifty years, only has good words about Ben. 'He was really a very kind young man,' she says. 'If I wanted anything, if I was out of anything, and if they were going shopping, they'd always ask me. He [Ben] even took me to the doctor's.' She adds that she was friends with Ben's grandparents and had enjoyed watching the grandchild of the former tenants begin his own family. 'He was very fond of that little girl,' she recalls.

Another neighbour tells me that Ben helped arrange the installation of new mailboxes for all four apartments in the building. Then she makes a curious claim. She believes she saw people watching the apartment block when Ben last lived there: 'There was a car with people sitting in it all the time, every morning at seven o'clock.' I already know that in late 2009, Australian intelligence agents followed Ben on the streets of Melbourne, but I'm not sure they would have been that obvious a presence on his street. The neighbour admits that she may have been influenced by her avid reading of the coverage of Ben's life.

For much of Ben and Haya's final year in Melbourne, it seemed that they were living a good life. Their circumstances were made easier by the fact that they didn't have to pay rent because their apartment was owned by the Zygier family. 'Money just didn't seem to be an issue,' says one friend. This was despite neither Ben nor Haya having any obvious paid employment, although it is likely that Ben was still receiving a salary from the Mossad, which allows for paid study leave. The extended family was flourishing too. Ben's parents would've been pleased that their son was home and that they now had a grandchild. They would've been further cheered when Ben's sister graduated from her social work degree at Melbourne University, intent on using her new skills to try to make the world a better place.

On the surface, Ben was a relatively carefree part-time graduate student, whose morning routine involved going to the gym with a few friends, often followed by breakfast at a cafe. But there were signs that his secret life in Israel had left its mark. The most obvious was that Ben barely ate. His friends ordered heartily after a gym session, but Ben did not. 'He had problems with food,' says one friend. There were hints that Ben denied himself food as punishment for some unspoken mistake. His friends thought it was related to guilt over the deaths of his fellow soldiers in 1997 or—at least to those aware of it—the pressure of the secret career that he never spoke openly about.

The friends he mixed with in Melbourne had known him as a teenager; they knew he'd always been a little unpredictable. But now, at age thirty-two, he had mood swings that caught even his friends by surprise. Having long bounced back and forth between Australia

The King David School in Melbourne, where Ben Zygier spent his primary school years. (Photo © Mark Hanlin)

The Hashomer Hatzair youth club, one of a number of Zionist youth organisations in Melbourne. (Photo © Mark Hanlin)

Ben Zygier, second from right, during a youth camp in the 1980s.
(Photo © Rafael Epstein)

The author as a young man on a hike in Galilee, holding an AR-15 assault
rifle borrowed from a security guard. (Photo © Rafael Epstein)

A member of the Jewish burial society searches for human remains among the wreckage of the crash of two Israeli transport helicopters that killed 73 soldiers, some of them friends of Ben Zygier. (AP Photo/Yaron Kaminsky)

Meir Dagan, Director of Mossad, the Israeli Institute for Intelligence and Special Operations, during Ben Zygier's service.(AP Photos/Dan Balilty, File)

Ben Zygier during his national service. (Photo supplied)

Ayalon prison in Ramle near Tel Aviv, the jail where Ben Zygier was secretly held. (AFP Photo/Jack Guez)

Ben Zygier is featured on the front page of Israeli newspaper *Maariv*. (AP Photo/Bernat Armangue)

and Israel, Ben had not always found it easy to maintain friendships. Now that he was back in Melbourne, he sought to rebuild many connections, drawing people in closely and surprising them with his trademark spur-of-the-moment, funny phone calls. But then Ben might suddenly snarl at someone when an unplanned phone call came back his way. Someone who found Ben too unpredictable to restore the closeness of the past gave this brutal assessment: 'He was a pretty polarising character, Ben. You sort of loved him or you hated him and you could never really trust him.'

It wasn't just those who'd known him at school who noticed his discontent. Despite the recollections of many of his neighbours in Caulfield, Ben was not always a calm or considered presence at home. 'He wasn't very focused. He'd come in ... speak on the phone, leave again,' says one woman who was familiar with Ben's family. Like many young people, Ben was often attached to his phone and seemed heavily dependent on it. Many people I speak with relate having broken conversations with Ben because he was consistently distracted by phone calls. Whoever was on the other end of the call seemed to take precedence over exchanges with friends and acquaintances. 'He didn't engage with what we were doing ... he wasn't a relaxed person,' says a friend who spent time with Ben's family.

One reason for this may have been unresolved tension between Ben and Haya over which country they would finally call home. To their friends, this was evident in the fact that their young daughter was pre-enrolled at Ben's former primary school, The King David, but he really wanted her to go to Bialik, the more Zionist school where he had finished Year 12. Ben was keen to return to Israel, but Haya was apparently not convinced that was the best idea. 'She was really happy here. She wanted to be here for a while. She was not rushing back to Israel,' says a friend of hers. Another factor was that the couple wanted to grow their family. 'Haya was also very aware of Ben's mother not having any other grandchildren and I got the impression that she was trying to work out how to stay here,' says the friend.

But it was hard for Haya to contemplate a long-term future in Australia. 'Her parents were in Israel and she didn't want them to get upset about it, because they made *aliyah*,' says another friend. In previous decades, people who had left Israel for good were accused of *yerida*, which literally means 'stepping down' or 'going lower'. The social taint of such a move may have dissipated by 2009, but Haya may still have feared her parent's disapproval of her departure from the country they'd chosen. Haya may also have known that if Ben remained connected to the Mossad, Israel was the only real option for where they could live.

It was not a given that Ben would continue working with the agency. The Mossad probably didn't keep close tabs on Ben when he was in Melbourne—he'd been allowed to go to Australia to study, to have a break and consider what he'd like to do next. But several people tell me that the Mossad was on Ben's mind a lot during this period, that he thought deeply about whether to continue his career, that he wanted to rethink the direction his life had taken.

While Ben said very little to his family and close friends about the Mossad, it seems he said a lot more to his fellow students at the Caulfield campus of Monash University, only a few minutes' drive from his apartment. Although his Master of Management classmates were unfamiliar to him, he was good at making friends with strangers—some of his friends tell me he was better at talking with strangers than he was at maintaining relationships with his friends. It was this friendliness towards other students, which at first seemed like Ben's usual willingness to mix with others, that tipped into risky behaviour.

The Heart of the Secret

Ben's mistake was a simple one and lacked the determination and intent that has been suggested in the media. In Israel, the term used for Ben's crime is *hasood*, 'the secret'. More tantalisingly, it is sometimes described as *livat hasood*, or 'the heart of the secret'. Put simply, Ben said too much to the wrong person at the wrong time.

There were a number of overseas students in the management course, including people from Malaysia and Saudi Arabia. Significantly for Ben, there was also a businessman who had links to Iran, and it was this Iranian who played a key role in Ben's downfall.

From what I can gather, Ben had been a reasonably successful agent for the Mossad, performing well in Iran and other places. But he was clearly in a fragile state, so his judgement may simply have deserted him. Establishing precisely what he did is difficult because the Mossad is so secretive about this, but my understanding is that Ben began talking about things he should not have ever discussed, not only telling people that he used to work for the Mossad but divulging details of the operations against Iran in which he'd been personally involved. It seems incomprehensible that someone who'd received Mossad training and was so committed to Israel would do this. He must have understood it was dangerous to talk about such things. Yet two sources tell me that's what Ben did in conversations at the university, including with the Iranian businessman. This man is described to me as being 'unscrupulous', which makes Ben's willingness to disclose important facts to him even more surprising.

Ben did not have a senior role in the operations that targeted Iran. But it didn't matter. He had been to Tehran, he had backed up his senior colleague from the communications company in Milan, and he knew plenty about what the Mossad was trying to do. His loose talk was a serious problem, especially as the program of assassination of Tehran scientists was then near its peak. Even just the leaking of Ben's name and the name of the Italian company where he had worked potentially could have been disastrous. Simply tracking his movements in and out of Tehran using his passport details, determining who Ben had met with, could have exposed many Iranians to dangerous scrutiny as would-be Israeli informants. The sources who confirm this version of Ben's central mistake will not spell out the details of what Ben said, but they tell me it was significant enough to get Ben's erratic behaviour flagged in Tel Aviv, and for the Mossad to begin an investigation.

After cross-checking various facts and details, I have come to believe that the Iranian businessman knew that what he was hearing was valuable, and relayed the information back to Iran. Tehran's security services started talking with the Iranian about the Mossad agent, and the details revealed by Ben then became part of the electronic traffic between Tehran and a European capital city—probably in an effort to find out more about what Ben had done in Europe. This traffic was then picked up by the massive surveillance network operated by Israel's Unit 8200.

Unit 8200 has some of the best signal-interception equipment in the world, technology that has played a crucial role in the work conducted by the National Security Agency.[2] Two technology companies founded in Israel—Narus and Verint—developed some of the software that the NSA uses to vacuum up vast quantities of internet traffic. Scanning high-bandwidth 'pipes', the software can identify a few packets of interest among billions of pieces of useless information, even as they race along at incredible speeds. Emails can be reconstructed, along with their attachments, and voice calls over the internet can be pieced back together to be analysed for their content.

It comes as no surprise, then, that when Ben blabbed in Melbourne, the Mossad heard about it in Tel Aviv via Tehran. And Ben's chatter was serious enough to bring the full weight of the security state down on his shoulders.

Some who knew Ben could not think of him as someone who took life seriously enough to be trusted by any government with the secrets that are the daily grist of espionage. 'It almost reminded me of some sort of game that he was playing … No-one really took him seriously,' says a woman who knew Ben over the last five years of his life. Another woman's memory of Ben's attitude to life is even less flattering: 'He [was] all talk. He was just really up himself and thinks he's great and he works for the army and that sort of thing.'

It's hard to know if people's recollections of Ben represent his true character, a front he sometimes displayed, a mistaken observation or a glimpse of a significant character flaw. What seems certain is that he was wildly inconsistent in what he revealed to different friends and members of his family. I'm told that some of his closest friends did not know he worked for the Mossad until after he died, while others knew who he worked for and in which countries he was stationed—I'm even told Ben was telling acquaintances in Israel about where he worked as soon as he began his training.

From all that I have been told about Ben's restlessness, his agitation and his consideration of a future outside of the Mossad, it is clear to me that by 2009 he was under significant psychological pressure. It may simply have been that his natural tendency to swing between exuberance and anger, to oscillate between being quietly retiring and outwardly happy, began to be noticed more and more by those around him. If so, few people seem to have recognised his behaviour for what it was. I believe that he was under a lot of pressure to reimagine his future and that this clouded his ability to think clearly. Perhaps that confusion is what caused him to blurt out the words that several months later led him to a jail cell.

The Last Happy Occasion

Late one Saturday night in October 2009, while he was at home in Caulfield, Ben Zygier sent his wife an email. It was an invitation to their young daughter's birthday party, and Ben was pretty pleased with how it looked. Beneath a cute picture of their daughter was a simple request: 'Please join us to celebrate Naomi's 2nd birthday!' This was followed by a date in November and the address of Ben's parents' comfortable home in nearby Malvern. The final line of the invitation read: 'Looking forward to seeing you! Haya, Ben & Naomi.' This husband-to-wife message was an just an ordinary task Ben was finishing off on just another Saturday night. But the subject of the invitation would be one of the last family gatherings that Ben ever attended, the last happy occasion before his family's life fell apart.

Two months later the Mossad told Ben that he needed to return to Israel, and while he wasn't sure exactly why his return was required, he could tell his employer was concerned about him—this in turn became a source of tension between him and Haya. What he didn't know was just how much of an intelligence operation his own life had become. Rather than having a discrete year off in Melbourne, he was being carefully assessed by the Israeli agency that had groomed him. And unbeknown to either Ben or the Mossad, Australia's domestic intelligence service, ASIO, had also begun to secretly monitor Ben's life.

Ben's friends were mostly in the dark too, although some had their suspicions. When news of Ben's imminent return to Israel broke, the trip's uncertain timing and purpose were simply another indication that he was involved in clandestine work. After all, for several years he had been unwilling to speak frankly or in detail about what he'd been doing, and then he'd suddenly arrived back in Australia and had seemed to be both busy and at a loose end, frustrated by a lack of purpose. 'He kind of had a lot of time and that's what didn't make sense,' says one friend. 'What was he doing studying?'

Ben's supposed overseas trips in 2009 had only added to the intrigue. He told some of the people he studied with that he was travelling in his role as a consultant in Geneva with a global consulting firm. But it turned out that no such firm existed in Switzerland. Some of his neighbours remember Ben telling them that he was going to visit Israel but he brought no Israeli publications back with him. It was only after these neighbours learned who Ben had worked for that they wondered if he'd really been to Israel at all.

Those closest to him preferred not to ask what was going on, although they speculated among themselves. Rumours circulated about the holiday in Egypt when the British couple Ben had befriended died in an accident. The story of the chopper crash also loomed large. There were even whispers of children or other soldiers being accidentally killed on one of Ben's army operations in Lebanon. But no-one confronted Ben about the reality of his work or what had actually happened in his life. Some of his friends liken it to the way the'dy learned to relate to those Jews who'd survived the horrors of World War II. 'It's like Holocaust survivors. You don't ask them what happened, do you? You wait for them to open up,' says one friend who was happy not to intrude on the hidden aspects of Ben's life.

Soon after Naomi's birthday party had taken place, when it emerged that Ben and Haya needed to return to Tel Aviv, the couple were vague about the reason for the trip, its duration and when they might depart. 'They were saying they wanted to go to Israel,' says someone close to them, 'but she [Haya] didn't really want to go because Naomi was about to start kinder, and they kept putting off going.' Another friend alludes to the pressure that was probably exerted by the Mossad: 'It wasn't necessarily that Ben wanted to return to Israel but he may have had to.'

None of the couple's friends knew, but Haya was also pregnant for the second time. Before she and Ben left for what they both hoped would be a quick trip to Israel, the biggest decision Haya thought she faced was whether she could persuade her husband to stay in Australia, and what she'd tell her parents if that happened. She couldn't have known that her husband would only ever get to see his second child inside a jail cell. She couldn't have had any conception of the composure she would need over the next twelve months, or of the massive secret she would have to keep.

Out of the Blue

A month after his daughter's birthday party, Ben was accused of being a spy by someone he'd never met. Worse still, the accusation came from a journalist. The surprise mobile call came from the then Jerusalem correspondent for *The Age* and *The Sydney Morning Herald*, Jason Koutsoukis. 'It wasn't a very long conversation, probably five minutes at the most, and his reaction was just bafflement,' Koutsoukis tells me. He says he asked Ben straight out if he worked for the Mossad, and that Ben had responded, 'That's a total fantasy.'

Ben's secret work life had been leaked by an old Canberra-based acquaintance of Koutsoukis, a man he's always presumed works for Australia's intelligence community. Out of the blue, this acquaintance had contacted Koutsoukis while he was in Israel and said: 'Look, we've got a story for you. Is there some way we can … communicate which is more secure than just the telephone?' Like most people who pass on classified information to journalists, this source wanted there to be no electronic footprint. 'He was very concerned about security, so we worked out that we could email each other in a particular way,' Koutsoukis tells me.

The email he received was journalistic dynamite. It blandly revealed that 'intelligence investigations have uncovered one particular Israeli agent of Australian birth who is currently living back in Australia'. It was the first time Ben's intelligence work was discussed outside the secretive confines of a security service. The email also contained allegations that turned out not to be true, such as 'the suspicion that he [Ben] is involved in an active Mossad operation in this country [Australia]'.

While tracking down Zygier's mobile number among the Australians in Jerusalem, Koutsoukis says he had to be fairly discreet because 'I didn't want it to get around that I'm chasing this weird story that Ben's a Mossad agent'. He had doubts about the story, particularly as 'it wasn't the first time someone had suggested a story like this to me'. But this was no outlandish yarn. Koutsoukis didn't know it at the time, but he had very deliberately been given access to a wider investigation that had been run out of ASIO's green-glassed Melbourne headquarters. What he received were not small scraps of intelligence, or by-products of a wider but unrelated operation, but details of a significant security effort.

Sandwiched between other offices in a 34-storey office block in Melbourne's CBD is a level dubbed the 'spooks floor'. Officially, it is referred to as the Attorney-General's Department, because that is who has responsibility for ASIO. The organisation's Melbourne office is dwarfed by its massive new building in Canberra and by its Sydney headquarters, but nonetheless it is usually kept busy looking at the fringes of the city's Islamic community or providing security assessments to help protect Melbourne's schools. Sometimes, the work it does also feeds into Australia's overseas intelligence efforts in places like Africa. Keeping an eye on an Australian working for Israeli intelligence is not an everyday occurrence here, but since the New Zealand passport factory had been uncovered in 2004, ASIO had been preparing for breaches like this.

From July 2009, ASIO had conducted an operation that looked at the activities of Ben and two other Australian Jews who had earlier moved to Israel and were now suspected of being Mossad agents. It was this characterisation that Koutsoukis' sources seemed intent on publicising. They appeared to want to convey to the journalist that all three men had repeatedly received new Australian passports under different names, which allowed them to travel internationally on behalf of the Mossad. Koutsoukis would later report the claim that they journeyed to countries that were hostile to Israel and where passports from the Jewish state were not welcome, like Lebanon, Syria and Iran.

The names on Ben's passports were mostly legitimate. In one, Ben had used the surname Burrows, a small tribute to his close friend Dan Burrows. In another, he'd used the name Alon, which was the surname that appeared on the invitation to Naomi's birthday party—this was Ben and Haya's adopted surname in Israel and it was also the name Ben had studied under in 2009. It is not illegal for an individual to have different Australian passports. Australians can change the name on their passport once every twelve months under a law introduced in 2004, coincidentally just after Ben began his Mossad career. 'This is unbelievable! What a resource for Mossad,' says one Israeli source. He suggests that any Australian-born citizen who is recruited to work for Israeli intelligence can enter a country like Syria or Lebanon under a different name each year. However, it is clearly a breach of Australian law to use one of the country's passports while working as a spy for the Mossad.

An investigation like the one that appears to have targeted Ben would have required a significant number of ASIO officers and staff. From what Koutsoukis says, it seems the intelligence organisation listened to Ben's phone calls and followed him on the streets of

Melbourne. They knew he was telling tales he should not have about his exploits in the Mossad. Koutsoukis says Ben was 'telling people he went to Iran while he was in Australia doing his master's. I think the Australians were listening to him and that's how they got that impression.'

The information provided to Koutsoukis didn't stop flowing with the tip-off that initiated that first conversation with Ben in December 2009. He says that soon after that phone call, his contacts had more for him, the sort of information a journalist could never hope to dig up on their own. Koutsoukis says they gave him the name of the satellite communications company in Milan for which Ben had worked—something the journalist quickly verified—mistakenly believing it to be a Mossad front designed to infiltrate Iran. This showed that the Australian intelligence community knew a fair bit about the Mossad's covert use of what turned out to be a legitimate business. The information they gave to Koutsoukis was comprehensive. Ben's passports were said to be full of Iranian entry visas, while his more senior Mossad colleague had visas in his passports from trips to Syria, Iran, Egypt and Dubai. Mention was also made of a third Australian who had Iranian entry and exit stamps in his passport, and who during one trip in 2004 had sought help from the Australian consulate in Tehran.

Still, in that first phone call with Ben Zygier, Koutsoukis says he thought the alleged spy's denials seemed genuine: 'He just said, "Well, that's total bullshit" and "Be on your way."' Ben was believably incredulous: 'You must have me confused with someone else.' Koutsoukis says he was flummoxed: 'I thought he was very convincing, and I thought, gee, you know, I believe him. What am I doing?'

An Act of Unusual Bastardry

The phone call from Koutsoukis would have stunned Ben—when you are a spy and a journalist knows who you are, your undercover purpose has become redundant. Ben's first concern must have been who had found out about his involvement in the Mossad and told Koutsoukis. He also may have wondered if these events were connected to his imminent return to Israel. Perhaps he became concerned that what he had been saying to his fellow students at his university campus had finally gotten back to the wrong people, and that maybe this information had ended up with the media. But it was unlikely that he was aware that Australia's intelligence agencies were involved in this mess.

ASIO and the Mossad are allies. They share the same goals in the Middle East. They share information gained from the work that the Mossad does in its region, intelligence that Australia could never hope to acquire itself. Blowing Ben's cover would have been an act of unusual bastardry by a supposedly friendly intelligence agency.

I try to get ASIO to confirm that it, or someone else in Australia's intelligence community, did this and to explain why information was passed on to Koutsoukis. 'Always go through the front door first' is the advice I'm given by a national security source in Australia. So I contact ASIO's media office, and after speaking with an officer who won't give me his name, I email my request to ASIO Director-General David Irvine. I want to at least explain what I have learnt so far. A month later, I receive a rather desultory response:

RE: Request from Rafael Epstein, ABC [SEC=UNCLASSIFED, CAVEAT=FOR-OFFICIAL-USE-ONLY]

10 May 2013 4.12pm
Good afternoon Mr Epstein.

Apologies for the delay in responding to you on this matter.

The Director-General asked that we pass on a thank you for the opportunity, however he politely declines.

Regards,
ASIO Media Liaison

The knock-back is unsigned.

It's reasonable to assume that ASIO mounted an investigation into Ben, given the New Zealand passport experience and the expulsion soon after of Amir Laty. Australia and Israel even had a formal agreement that their spies would not use each other's passports. But I still have no official confirmation of this investigation.

Physical surveillance cannot be casually undertaken because it requires a large team of people. When the target is being trailed, whoever is physically close to the subject being followed has to move away at regular intervals and hand over to someone else. Tracking someone properly can involve up to eight vehicles full of trained personnel. A base of operations also needs to be set up, often within a kilometre of the suspect's home. All of this can generate a salary bill in the tens of thousands of dollars. In addition, while ASIO doesn't need a court order to listen to someone's phone calls, tapping Ben's phone would have required a letter signed by the federal Attorney-General. ASIO would then have had a legal obligation to inform the Attorney-General how the phone taps had assisted its investigation. So if what Koutsoukis tells me is true, ASIO had seen fit to mount a significant operation.

I also struggle to understand why ASIO or any other part of Australia's intelligence apparatus would decide to leak Ben's name. ASIO benefits from Israel's focus on Iran, and Tel Aviv works closely with Washington to contain Iran's nuclear ambitions. By exposing Ben, ASIO was risking the exposure of a Mossad operation, not just a Mossad agent. Intelligence agencies often have to make decisions many would consider unethical, but speaking to the media about Ben was unusually aggressive, especially considering there were other, more private ways in which ASIO could have vented its anger to Israel at Ben's activities. Some people who are familiar with ASIOs work assure me that this is something the organisation would never do.

Desperate to find out if and why ASIO or another Australian agency has done this, I decide on a new approach that I suspect will draw a response. I have been given the name of a senior ASIO figure, the result of a complex, risky process—you can't just Google an organisational chart of ASIO, and there is the possibility that even mentioning the name of such an individual to someone else constitutes a criminal offence. I don't want to simply email this man, so I visit the ASIO office in Melbourne. The concierge has clearly been instructed to deflect such queries, so first I have to persuade him that I know ASIO has facilities in the building. He then concedes that I can drop off a letter explaining that I'd like to speak to the ASIO officer.

A few weeks later, I have still not received a reply to my note. So I try calling the number published on ASIO's webpage, thinking I might have more success this way. When I ask to speak with the senior ASIO officer, a male voice tells me to wait one moment, using a casual tone that suggests I'll shortly be put through. But there is a silence that goes on for so long that I am certain they will hang up. Eventually the voice returns, although the tone is less casual now, perhaps reflecting concern about who I am and how I know the name of any ASIO officer, let alone someone high up in one of its biggest offices. After a brief exchange, I am put on hold again, left to hope—in vain, as it turns out—that I will now be put in touch with the officer. In the end, the voice merely agrees to take a message.

I never receive a formal answer to the question of whether, and if so why, ASIO handed Ben's identity over to Koutsoukis, although I am eventually told by one source that ASIO had indeed put Ben under considerable surveillance. I ask Jason Koutsoukis why he thought he had been the recipient of the information. 'These two guys [Australian intelligence operatives] thought, here are some Australians and they're kind of manipulating our system a little bit so that they can work for Israeli intelligence, and they didn't like it,' Koutsoukis tells me. 'I think that they felt that their complaints weren't being heard within Canberra, and they wanted to blow the whistle on it … I think they were just acting completely on their own and with no authority from anybody.'

Why any member of Australia's intelligence community would want to speak to a reporter rather than directly with Tel Aviv is difficult to fathom. However, people who work with classified information do sometimes decide, impulsively or with aforethought, to talk to journalists. From police to members of the intelligence community, individuals release classified information to further specific agendas. Some 'leakers' are authorised to act in this way without having to seek explicit permission. Others leak because they know their superiors would want this detail in the public domain without being responsible for sanctioning the release of the information. Some even do it to spite their bosses. And sometimes information is leaked for reasons that are barely discernible, if at all, to those outside the organisation. As a journalist, I've published stories based on information provided by multiple sources where I still do not understand why that information was directed to me.

A few weeks after Ben was told by the Mossad that he needed to go back to Israel, that agency and ASIO would share concerns about the use of Australian passports in a high-profile assassination in Dubai. But before that happened, Ben most likely would have told the Mossad about the phone call from an Australian journalist. 'It was such a weird thing that he gets a call from a journalist asking if he is a Mossad agent,' Koutsoukis tells me, 'so I think he must have told them—I just can't believe he didn't. And that must have given them cause for concern.'

PRISONER

A Chaotic Nexus

By late December 2009, the calls from Tel Aviv had likely become more urgent as the Mossad tried to persuade Ben to return to Israel without revealing the depth of its concerns. I believe that at this time, Ben still thought that if he just spoke with his handlers, he would be able to straighten things out. He probably thought he could talk his way out of any difficulty, because he always had before. I don't think he knew the agency was investigating whether he'd leaked secrets. This explains why he seems to have planned on staying in Israel only a short time—in early January 2010, when Ben and his family suddenly left Australia, they left behind a flat that was still full of important documents, furniture, clothes, toys and other possessions. However, in reality, it would be months before Haya returned, by which time her husband would be in jail.

Ben didn't tell most of his family or close friends about the trip to Israel. 'It was kind of weird,' says one friend. 'One day we were told, "Oh, they've gone for a couple of weeks."' Another friend says, 'They left and we didn't get to say goodbye. I thought, "I'll just see them when they get back," and I kept asking, "When are they back? When are they back?" ... I remember being surprised that they'd gone back to Israel when they did because it seemed so close to the beginning of the school year.'

Soon after Ben had flown from the heat of a Melbourne summer into a mild Israeli winter, Jason Koutsoukis again called him on his mobile phone. This time, says Koutsoukis, Ben sounded angry: 'Who the fuck are you and what is this total bullshit you are telling me?' He seemed shocked by the suggestion he was under surveillance. 'I have never been to any of those countries that you say I have been to,' Ben had said. 'I am not involved in any kind of spying. That is ridiculous.'[1] Reflecting on this conversation three years later, Koutsoukis tells me that Ben actually seemed more frustrated than angry: 'He was really rude to me. But I had that feeling you get when you're trying to get an interview and you've tried one too many times, and then they just get pissed off with you and they say, "Listen, just leave me alone."'

Ben would've been rattled by the phone call from Koutsoukis. He also would have spoken with his managers at the Mossad by this point and would have known he was in trouble, though not how much. Ben was telling friends he would be in Israel for longer than he anticipated, that he had more unspecified work to do. I imagine this led to a conversation in Raanana with Haya during which he tried to explain to her what was going on and admitted that he couldn't tell her when they'd be able to return to Australia. I picture Ben and Haya walking around the park in the middle of their suburb, talking about what they could or should do. And as he and Haya fretted and speculated about what had gone wrong, less than an hour's drive away, Mossad officers were gathering evidence that would lead to his arrest.

The Mossad was so concerned about who Ben had spoken to in Melbourne, and what he may have revealed, that it called in the Israel Security Agency, known in Hebrew as the Sherut ha'

Bitachon ha'Klali, but better known by the acronym Shabak or Shin Bet. This was a serious escalation of the situation—the Shin Bet is normally associated with intrusive investigations into Palestinian communities, but it also deals with the rarer eventuality of an Israeli agent suspected of betraying the state. However, while the senior ranks of the Mossad faced the very unpleasant arrest of one of their own agents, this was balanced by the prospect of a complex hit in Dubai. As the evidence against Ben was compiled in one part of the Mossad, another section was tracking the agents who'd left Israel for the small Gulf state of Dubai, on a mission to kill the Palestinian arms dealer Mahmoud al-Mabhouh.

Two days after news of al-Mabhouh's assassination caused a global media frenzy, the Shin Bet finally made its move against Ben. Its officers knocked on Ben's door in Raanana on the morning of 31 January 2010 and took him to an interrogation room in Tel Aviv. There, Ben was told what he had most feared—he had been arrested for speaking about sensitive Mossad matters.

Jason Koutsoukis and Ronen Bergman later reported that when Ben was arrested, he had a DVD filled with classified information in his possession. But this detail could have been given to the journalists to imply that Ben had planned to reveal even more Mossad secrets. From what I know, this is not as rare an occurrence as intelligence agencies such as the Mossad would like it to be. I've encountered others who work with classified files and who have made unauthorised copies of them.

The Dubai assassination that coincided with Ben's arrest produced a chaotic nexus of recrimination, revelation and confusion. Some of Ben's friends couldn't reach him on the phone, so they assumed he'd had a role in the Dubai murder and had gone into hiding. It seemed to confirm their long-held suspicion that Ben worked for Israeli intelligence. Otherwise, why would he not respond to their emails, and why the sudden silence from Haya? The concern among Ben's friends grew when they heard that his mother, Louise, was making an unplanned trip to Israel. The lack of information fuelled frustration, then anger. 'I remember Daniel

[Burrows] getting really angry with Ben because he couldn't get hold of him and his phone was cut off and he was really pissed off,' a friend tells me.

Some in Ben's extended family began asking the questions they'd never openly voiced. One friend of Ben's says he was asked, 'Has Haya ever said anything to you about [the] Mossad?' In the wake of Ben's sudden disappearance, the refrain from his family also became 'We think he was involved in Dubai.' The assassination, splashed prominently across TV screens and news websites, was just the sort of operation Ben had dreamed of being involved in. But instead he was facing a tough interrogation and the prospect of years in jail.

As soon as Ben was taken into custody, Haya's life changed irrevocably. The short trip to Israel had morphed into a nightmare. She doggedly tried to work out precisely what accusations Ben faced, but she was told very little, and her communications with her husband were strictly monitored. It was a cataclysmic change in her circumstances that she had to handle on her own, while looking after one child and being three months pregnant with another. And there was little she could share with those back in Melbourne. One of Ben's cousins was sent by Haya to the Caulfield flat to retrieve files from a home computer and send them to Israel. No-one understood why Haya needed such documents immediately, nor why Ben was suddenly 'off the grid'. When the cousin was asked for an explanation, her response was glum: 'She's not telling me what she needs them for. I'm just doing whatever she's asking me to do.'

To the Mossad, the man killed in Dubai had been an important target. Though the world often thinks of the agency as constantly eliminating Israel's enemies, it is thought to have been behind as few as thirty assassinations.[2] But it is the perception of many more deaths that has Israel's potential targets wasting time and resources second-guessing themselves. Hundreds have been killed in the Palestinian territories and in Lebanon by aerial strikes, car bombs and other explosives, but these were mostly not Mossad-led operations. The operation in Dubai, however, required a significant number of the organisation's best-trained people, those from the unit inside Caesarea called Kidron, which means 'spear'. Kept separate from most others at the Mossad and subjected to the toughest of physical and psychological testing and schooling, these were the agents Ben Zygier had read about as a boy and wanted to emulate. But as the first members of the Kidron kill team flew into Dubai on 18 January, Ben's Mossad career was already over.

Unnatural Causes

Early on the morning of 19 January 2010, the final group of Israeli spies began arriving at the international airport in the Gulf city-state of Dubai. As the day unfolded, the Israeli agents spread out across the city, joining other members of the Mossad team who'd arrived the day before.

The Al Maktoum family rules this gleaming desert metropolis as an absolute monarchy. But it is a place where everybody is welcome. It's like Vienna at the height of the Cold War, a crossroads for spies, diplomats, arms traders and terrorists-cum-freedom fighters. This tiny country is a haven for covert work, ideal for dubious deeds done in the shadows, a realm that strikes a delicate balance between what is publically deplored but privately permitted. The CIA has a presence here, as do strongmen, former warlords and shady political operatives from around the region. Even the Australian Army is here, stationed in the desert at the Al Minhad Air Base, where hundreds of NATO Coalition troops work to back up operations in places like Afghanistan. But Australian journalists visiting this base are told not to mention the country in which they've landed. That information is part of a foreign footprint that the ruling royal family is keen to keep out of the public eye.

Along with the spooks, soldiers and militants, another frequent visitor to Dubai was the Palestinian Mahmoud al-Mabhouh, an arms dealer for Hamas tagged on the Mossad's assassination list with the randomly generated codename 'Plasma Screen'.[3] On 19 January, in the middle of the afternoon, al-Mabhouh arrived on Emirates flight 912 from Damascus. He was closely followed by Israeli agents as he took a taxi from the airport to the five-star Al Bustan Rotana, where he checked in. He asked for a room with no balcony—the door that opened into the corridor was the only way in.

Around twenty-four hours later, the door of al-Mabhouh's room was forced open by hotel staff who were concerned that no-one answered when they telephoned and knocked. The initial death certificate said he suffered a brain haemorrhage. His hotel door was latched from the inside, so the conclusion was that he died of natural causes. But when the authorities in Dubai realised who the victim was, they looked at the incident more closely. And looking was precisely what they were well equipped to do.

Dubai is saturated with surveillance cameras, to an extent matched by few other cities in the world. The autocratic emirate very publicly decided to use CCTV to monitor what goes on within its borders. More than 1500 camera sites are run by the country's police, who also have access to many more private cameras. And around the time of al-Mabhouh's murder, they put them to good use. They'd recently caught the killer of a high-profile Lebanese pop star with the help of video recordings, and cameras had also captured Russian agents shooting dead a former Chechen rebel leader as he sat in one of Dubai's car parks. According to a secret cable later sent by US diplomats in Dubai back to Washington, and circulated by WikiLeaks, the local police had tired of others using their city as a killing ground:

> Al Mabhouh's killing was the third high-profile killing in Dubai over the past 18 months ... It has also been suggested to US Consulate officers that Dubai security personnel believe public embarrassment of Israel in this case will help Dubai fend off allegations by radical elements of complicity in the Mabhouh assassination.[4]

The Dubai coroner's initial impression that al-Mabhouh had died naturally from a brain haemorrhage had been reinforced by the trickle of blood found on the arms dealer's pillow. But prompted either by Hamas or the realisation that he had used a false passport, the Dubai police soon started doing serious detective work. They began by ploughing through the vast number of digital files recorded by their camera network. For nine days after al-Mabhouh's body was discovered, the police patiently sifted through this electronic haul of information, piecing together the preparation for the assassination and its aftermath, matching the CCTV vision with bank records, flight numbers and passport pictures. They also matched the footage to phone records and pinpointed a mobile phone company located in Vienna. The Israeli agents had all routed their mobile calls through the same European phone number, which made it easier for the police to trace the phones they'd used.

On 29 January, the head of the Dubai Police Force, General Dhahi Khalfan Tamim, dramatically publicised what had been discovered. Fronting a globally televised press conference, he directly accused the Mossad of killing Mahmoud al-Mabhouh. He even challenged the agency's boss, Meir Dagan, to 'be a man' and admit Israel's role in the murder. The subsequent release on YouTube of a half-hour stream of carefully edited CCTV footage, displaying the Mossad team in action, was not what Israel had expected, though it must have known about Dubai's extensive video surveillance network. This was followed over the next few days by reams of detailed information from the investigation.

It was not just the Mossad who was surprised. The United States was also taken aback, as recorded in the diplomatic cable released by WikiLeaks:

> The Dubai Police ... have demonstrated very publicly that their investigative capabilities exceed what was previously thought. Dubai officials likely hope that this public display of its talents (including a fascinating and professionally-produced YouTube video) will deter would-be assassins from using the Emirate to conduct business in the future.[5]

The YouTube video revealed almost every step of the carefully planned work of the Mossad's kill team. Over many hours, the members of the team were filmed arriving at the airport, booking into hotels, entering hotel lobby bathrooms and then emerging minutes later disguised with wigs and glasses, departing from a shopping mall where the police said they discussed the precision assassination that would follow, and watching al-Mabhouh check in to his hotel. The forensic detail revealed by the cameras was fascinating.

Some of the agents, wearing sports clothes and with towels around their necks and tennis rackets in hand, could be seen riding up in the same lift as al-Mabhouh after he'd checked in, apparently so they could confirm that he had stepped into room 230. Afterwards, they lingered in the hallway outside the room. One of the men then appeared to enter the number of al-Mabhouh's room and that of the one across the hallway, room 237, into his phone and send a text, before waiting to re-enter the lift. Minutes later, the men lingered outside the hotel, captured on yet another camera.

Twenty minutes later, a different agent called the Al Bustan Rotana from the lobby of another hotel and asked if room 237 was available. He booked it and then made another call, reserving a seat on a flight to Zurich that evening. This man then arrived at al-Mabhouh's hotel and checked in. But he never entered room 237, instead leaving both his briefcase and the room key with another agent in the lobby; he'd left the country by the time al-Mabhouh was killed.

After the arms dealer had left the hotel on some unknown errand, two of the team, thought to be those in charge, went separately to room 237, one at 4.45 p.m. and the other forty-five minutes later. At around 6.30 p.m., four other men arrived at the hotel wearing baseball caps—these were the men who would kill al-Mabhouh. Video footage showed that soon after, an innocent hotel guest disturbed the team close to room 230. But one of the assassins, who was wearing a hotel uniform, distracted the guest while the others presumably entered al-Mabhouh's room. Police later looked at the activity logged on the electronic door lock of the room and it showed that at 8 p.m., the Israeli agents either tried to reprogram the lock or used it to program their own electronic key.

At 8.24 p.m., al-Mabhouh returned to the hotel, waving casually to someone in the lobby. The Mossad agents were either waiting in his room or followed him into it soon after he arrived. The Dubai police said that al-Mabhouh was left lying under his sheets, dressed only in a pair of black shorts. Somehow, the Mossad team managed to lock the latch on the inside of room 230 so that the next day, staff would have to break it to open the door.

It was all done by 8.46 p.m. At that time, two of the four men with baseball caps were standing at the elevator, waiting to go back downstairs. They looked a little anxious, shifting back and forth as they waited for the lift. One telltale sign of what they'd done was the rubber glove on one man's hand, which he'd probably worn when killing al-Mabhouh. The other two men with baseball caps departed soon after.

Al-Mabhouh's body was released on 29 January, the same day the Dubai police broadcast their findings, and he was buried in a very public funeral in Damascus. The autopsy results took several more weeks to confirm, which invited scepticism in the Israeli press because al-Mabhouh had already been buried. The Dubai forensic lab said the dead man had a big bruise on his thigh where he'd been injected with a drug called succinylcholine. This is one of the fastest-acting muscle relaxants. Patients are rapidly paralysed, unable to move a muscle, but while they can't feel anything, they're still aware and conscious. The drug is often used as a general anaesthetic, commonly in emergency departments, and is sometimes used to euthanase large animals like horses. It can also cause a heart attack. Al-Mabhouh had more bruises on his nose, face and neck—the police said that after he was injected, he was smothered with a pillow.

When Dubai made its first very public announcement about al-Mabhouh's death, blaming the Mossad for it, there was one significant blank spot in the information they provided to the world. There were no published records nor any footage of what al-Mabhouh got up to in the hours before his death, while the

Mossad agents waited patiently at his hotel. Some reports claimed he met with those who fund and arm Hamas, which dovetailed with Israel's belief that the Dubai police wanted to protect the emirate's image as a squeaky clean centre for international business. Perhaps he just went shopping. When he was last seen in the hotel lobby, just before going up to his room for the last time, a bag containing a new pair of shoes was swinging by his side.

One of the First

In southern Israel, an off-duty policeman walks past a massive road sign at the Masmiya junction. He settles his revolver against his hip before crossing the road during a brief break in the fast-moving traffic. As he heads for the local McDonald's, he is passed by two women who are weaving their way around the many highway exits, their heads covered with scarves. Trucks litter the corner car park, their drivers taking a break and refuelling before following one of the roads that flow from here to Jerusalem, Tel Aviv, the southern city of Beersheva, which is close to the Gaza Strip, and the commuter town of Modi'in. The intersection is nondescript. I'm only here because in 1989—coincidentally the same year I spent in Israel—this is where a young, unsuspecting Israeli corporal called Ilan Saadoun hitched a ride with Mahmoud al-Mabhouh.

Israeli soldiers used to use intersections like this as hitchhiking centres almost as much as they would use public bus stops. During my year in Israel, my friends and I used to hitchhike too. As teenagers we were keen to travel the roads and explore the landscape of the country we were being encouraged to live in. Every junction like this used to have dozens of soldiers cadging lifts, so we'd sometimes imitate them, thinking if they were doing it, why not us too. But today at this junction, just 50 kilometres from Gaza, I see no hitchhiking soldiers, just drivers wolfing down scalding hot coffee bought from one of the ubiquitous Yellow Cafés that dot Israel's roads. The corner I'm on hosts only a few desultory palm trees, some cracked concrete blocks and big tray trucks carrying tractors.

Nearly a quarter of a century ago, Ilan Saadoun was one of the first Israeli soldiers to be targeted by the then fledgling militant group Hamas. Back then, Yasser Arafat's Palestine Liberation Organization was struggling to influence the first intifada, and Hamas was still finding its feet in the Gaza Strip. The militant Islamists wanted to make an impression. So al-Mabhouh and another man dressed up as Orthodox Jews, complete with skullcaps, and drove an old white Subaru with Israeli number plates to Masmiya junction. There, they pulled over and spoke to Ilan Saadoun and a friend of his, who were looking for a lift. Al-Mabhouh, who was driving, said he could fit only one passenger in the cramped back seat. To further discourage both men from jumping in, he also said one rear door was broken and couldn't be opened. Saadoun took the lift, farewelling his friend before the car drove off down the highway. Just minutes later, Saadoun was shot in the head. 'I heard him breathe heavily and die,' al-Mabhouh would later say.

The search for Saadoun instead turned up the body of another soldier who'd been missing for several months. Avi Sasportas was a special forces sergeant who had been killed in much the same way as Saadoun. Twenty-three years later, with Hamas entrenched in the Gaza Strip, al-Mabhouh would say of Sasportas, 'I wanted to shoot him, but Abu Suhaib [his partner] was faster than me. Sasportas took two bullets in the face and one in the chest and died from the first shot. His blood was all over the car.'[6]

The Israeli public responded to the killings with the very revulsion that Hamas had wanted to provoke. Israelis felt a visceral connection to the off-duty soldiers, who had probably been hitchhiking home to their loved ones. They wanted revenge for the deaths of men who could have been their sons, brothers or friends. The country focused its hatred on Hamas' wheelchair-bound spiritual leader Sheikh Ahmed Yassin, who was soon imprisoned.

For years after Saadoun's disappearance, every Israeli communication with Hamas demanded to know where the young corporal's body was buried. In 1996, his body was finally found. The following year, Sheikh Yassin was released from jail—he was eventually killed by a targeted Israeli Air Force strike in the Gaza Strip in 2004. As for al-Mabhouh, the Mossad trained its electronic eyes and ears on him for many years, and in 2010 they got their man in Dubai, just weeks before Ben's arrest in Tel Aviv.

Plundered Passports

By February 2010, the Dubai police were becoming known around the world for their neat schematic diagrams showing which Mossad agent had used which fake passport, documents purporting to be from countries such as Germany, France, Ireland and the United Kingdom. These revelations were not surprising. By definition, spies want to cover their tracks and they manufacture forged passports and other identity papers in order to do that. 'What we do is fundamentally illegal. We are there to steal secrets and break laws,' says David Manners, who used to run the CIA's station in Jordan in the 1990s. 'People say that we are like the FBI and I tell them, "No, the FBI are the cops, and we are the robbers."' What Manners means is that domestic agencies like ASIO and the FBI (Federal Bureau of Investigation) are responsible for ensuring that their nations' laws are enforced, and they rarely breach their own laws in pursuit of this goal. Overseas spy agencies like the CIA and the Mossad, however, have no laws to enforce. They are sent overseas to gather intelligence and they are expected to break laws to succeed at that task.

However, the disclosure about the passports did cause the Mossad some discomfort. The spies of the United States, United Kingdom and Australia can use fake passports from their own countries. But the Mossad has a unique problem. It cannot use its own passports, real or fake, in most of the nations it targets because these countries still refuse to recognise Israel's legitimacy. Iran, Syria and Lebanon don't accept Israeli nationals, and even when other Arab countries like Egypt do, Israeli citizens attract too much suspicion for intelligence work. This means that for decades, the Mossad has forged or borrowed (both with and without the owners' permission) the passports of other countries, something that has at turns worried, frustrated and exasperated these mainly Western nations.

For such a secret business, there has been some embarrassingly public exposure of what the Mossad has done. Sometimes this has led to the expulsion of Israeli diplomats and spies, and pledges to not repeat the practice. Countries cannot stop what they do not control, but Canada was notably absent from the list produced by the Dubai police.

The United States' nearest neighbour has long had to put up with having its passports plundered by foreign spy agencies. In 1940, when Leon Trotsky was stabbed to death with an ice pick in Mexico, his Soviet assassins used birth certificates stolen from dead Canadians. A stolen Canadian passport was also used by the Mossad agents who targeted Palestinians after the 1972 killing of Israelis at the Munich Olympics. In 1974, when a Palestinian militant was killed in Cyprus, the police in Nicosia seized another Canadian passport used by the Mossad, one that had come from a batch of fifty blank Canadian passports stolen from a bank vault in Vienna. But Israel's biggest humiliation in using Canadian identities occurred in Jordan in 1997. That botched mission illuminates much of what unfolded between Australia and Israel after the hit in Dubai and Ben's arrest.

After a wave of Hamas bombings in 1997, Israel made the hasty decision to go after a senior Hamas official called Khalid Mishal, who was living in Jordan. The plan was to unobtrusively spray an odourless poison into Mishal's ear, but the mission suffered from a lack of preparation. The two designated assassins failed to get close enough to Mishal because his daughter made an unexpected appearance at a crucial moment on the street in Amman. The would-be assassins fled but were soon surrounded by a jeering crowd of angry Jordanians and then arrested. The Mossad agents protested their innocence, insisting they were Canadian tourists. But Canadian diplomats who rushed to the assistance of the two men were perturbed when their offers of assistance were knocked back. The men's passports looked genuine, but the diplomats became suspicious when these supposed Canadians couldn't sing their national anthem or answer the most basic questions about the country, like recalling one of its best-known sporting teams—the Toronto Blue Jays. The pair were soon identified as Mossad agents. Their passports had been 'borrowed' from Canadian Jews living in Israel, an echo of Ben asking to borrow the passports of his friends in the mid-2000s. One of the genuine passport holders said he was just an 'innocent victim of some screwed up situation and I'd like it to go away'.[7]

The Mossad had to pay a high diplomatic price once its agents were exposed. 'We have an old saying in the business, that it's better to ask for forgiveness than for permission,' says Manners, who watched all this unfold in Amman. Using passports from another country is expected. 'We all know this happens,' says Manners. 'The unwritten rule is not to get caught.' He continues: 'The Mishal hit was very amateurish. In Dubai, while it was an impressive piece of police work after the fact to piece it all together, the fact is [the] Mossad got away with it—they made the hit and got out of the country.'

Among the initial batch of passports that the Dubai police claimed were used in the al-Mabhouh killing was just one genuine document, and it turned out that the Mossad had gone to great lengths to obtain it. In 2009, someone calling themselves Michael Bodenheimer applied for a passport and identity card in one of Germany's biggest cities, Cologne. Displaying his Israeli passport and what he said was his parents' marriage certificate, Bodenheimer claimed citizenship under a section of the German constitution specifically written to look after those hounded out of Germany by the Nazis. The Israeli passport was issued to Bodenheimer in 2008 and his German passport was issued in June 2009.[8]

The Dubai police believed that this man was in charge of communications for al-Mabhouh's assassination; he was presumably responsible for the SIM cards that came from the Austrian branch of the T-Mobile company, with the texts and calls made through an exchange in Vienna. It was determined by reporters from *Der Spiegel* that the addresses he had given to the passport authorities for his homes in Germany and Israel were not genuine: in Cologne, the nominated apartment block, located near a busy train station, had a high turnover of tenants; in Herziliya, the address was for an empty office in a business park, within walking distance of the Mossad's headquarters.

While Ben Zygier had been investigated by ASIO for his abuse of Australian passports, he had had nothing to do with Dubai. However, the explosive fact that the Mossad had misused Australia's passports in the operation was about to be announced by the police investigation in the secretive Gulf state.

A Secret Fate

In the days following Ben's arrest, he must have hoped his problem would soon sort itself out. But this would have been a denial of the seriousness of his situation. Initially, Shin Bet was so concerned about what Ben may have done that it did not want him communicating with anyone, keeping him isolated in a special interrogation facility. The investigators even went to a judge to argue he should be denied access to a lawyer. They believed his leaking of operational knowledge could significantly damage their operations in Iran and that he could not be trusted to speak to another person, including a legal representative. But court documents reveal the investigators lost their argument before a judge.

Haya, meanwhile, was thrust into new responsibilities. Instead of relying on Ben to navigate the strange world of Israeli espionage and national security, she was the one negotiating with lawyers and meeting with officials. Haya had been the one to call Ben's mother Louise to tell her the news of her son's arrest. She then began calling around to find out who could act as Ben's lawyer. 'She seems to hold it together,' says someone who knows her. 'She is really solid, very quiet, very reserved, very Australian in that way, not at all Israeli.'

Haya kept Ben's fate a secret from his closest friends. She communicated via the phone, Facebook and email without giving away the truth, faithfully protecting the fact that Ben had been jailed.

And she did so while the tensions that had previously existed between her and her husband were being intensely magnified by the possibility that Ben could be incarcerated for a very long time.

For several weeks after Ben's arrest, Australian officials reportedly did not know what had happened to him. Nor, apparently, had they yet been informed about the use of Australian passports in the death of al-Mabhouh. But this seems strange in light of the fact that in the first week of February 2010, Dubai sent Foreign Minister Sheikh Abdullah bin Zayed Al Nahyan on his first ever visit to Australia. The minister attended meetings in Canberra and an event organised by the Lowy Institute think tank in the Blue Mountains near Sydney. Many of the discussions centred on the importance of commercial relationships between Australia and Dubai, underlined by the statistic that more than 100 planeloads of Australians travel to Dubai each week, most on their way to another destination. But on the sidelines, away from the formal trade-related meetings, the effort by the Dubai police to embarrass the Mossad surely must have come up. It was the biggest event in the region at the time, due to both the assassination and the fury of countries like the United Kingdom and France over the Mossad's misuse of their passports.

When Australian Foreign Minister Stephen Smith was photographed with his Dubai counterpart, it was the sole media opportunity, but no questions were taken from journalists. Smith merely uttered simple pleasantries in the dull Canberra briefing room. He had good reason to be cautious. All countries need to choose their words carefully when speaking about Dubai, with seemingly unrelated issues often unexpectedly crashing over the top of each other. The Canadians learned about Dubai's sensitivities the hard way in November 2010, forced to shift their military operations to Cyprus after a trade row over access to airline routes. So with the news from Dubai making questions too difficult, Smith just mouthed a handful of words as photographers recorded the visit: 'The Sheikh and I both believe that we can get much more out of the relationship and we are very pleased with his visit.' There certainly would be much more to the relationship in the coming weeks.

Sixteen days after Ben's arrest, the Mossad decided that Australian authorities could finally be told about his arrest. But it was done in an unusual way: the news was relayed to one of ASIO's more senior officers. Normally, if an Australian citizen was arrested in Tel Aviv, the diplomats at the local Australian embassy would be told first. They would then be given access to the person in jail. But that didn't happen in Ben's case, and no-one from ASIO was sent to visit him inside his interrogation cell.

Australia's intelligence organisation realised that if it pushed too hard for a visit, it risked shutting down the fragile communication channel that Israel had just opened. Also, because the ASIO officer was senior and therefore unlikely to be lied to, when he was told that Ben was physically and mentally doing as best as could be expected, he accepted those assurances. But still, it was very strange that ASIO did not ask if it could speak to Ben to make sure that he had access to a lawyer and to check on his welfare. And it made this decision without telling a single senior minister, or alternatively conveying the news to the senior public servants who ran the government departments and reported directly to the ministers.

Not only was Ben an Australian citizen, but he'd been the subject of an ASIO investigation about the misuse of Australian passports. He had also been arrested at a time when the Mossad's passport forgery was a massive issue in the international media. But despite this swirl of controversies, ASIO waited another eight days after receiving the news of Ben's arrest before sharing it with those outside the organisation. And even then, ASIO only decided to share what it knew because Dubai had finally blown the whistle on the Mossad's use of Australian passports.

The Deepest Concern

Tuesday 23 February started normally enough for Foreign Minister Stephen Smith. Speaking at a Canberra press conference, he was unaware of the looming issues that would descend on his bureaucracy by that evening. Still, what he said had a connection to the outrage flowing out of Dubai. He announced a new regime of fingerprinting, retinal scans and digital photography that would be used to ensure people couldn't use fake passports. He said passport holders from more than ten countries would now have to submit to these new procedures to qualify for an Australian visa. It was part of a global trend that meant the Mossad and other intelligence agencies would have to work harder to procure passports for their spies.

At 9 p.m., Stephen Smith received a disturbing call from Australian officials in Dubai. As the emirate's police force had studiously added more names to its list of suspected Mossad agents, it had uncovered the use of three suspect Australian passports—a fourth would be added to the list a few weeks later. These documents had been explicitly linked to the assassination of Mahmoud al-Mabhouh, so the authorities in Dubai had alerted their Australian counterparts.

And there was an extra twist. Other passports used in the Mossad operation had involved concocted identities. Agents with Irish passports, for instance, used the fake names Kevin Daveron, Evan Dennings and Gail Folliard to swoop in and out of the emirate. But the names on the Australian passports all belonged to real people. The diagram neatly crafted by the Dubai police showed that an Australian woman called Nicole McCabe was one of those who followed al-Mabhouh. The other Australians, Adam Korman and Joshua Daniel Bruce, were likely part of a Mossad contingent present in Dubai in the lead-up to al-Mabhouh's murder, preparing for the assassination. Or perhaps they had been involved in an attempted hit on al-Mabhouh in Dubai a few months earlier.

After hearing the news from Dubai, Australian officials went into overdrive, furiously digging for information. They had to entertain the possibility that the three Australians were genuine Mossad agents, but after working through the night and then contacting the trio, they discovered this was not the case. The authentic passport photos had been replaced with doctored images of the agents who used them. There was, however, a remarkable coincidence. The three Australians had all been born in Melbourne and had later moved to Israel—just like Ben Zygier.

In that same furious period of quiet verification and diplomacy, Smith called Dubai's Foreign Minister to assure him that Australian authorities were 'fully cooperating' and that they took 'this matter very seriously'. Sheikh Abdullah bin Zayed Al Nahyan responded with a vow 'to bring those responsible to justice'. Meanwhile, inside ASIO, which had been involved in the search for the three passport holders, it was recognised that Ben's imprisonment and the use of Australian passports in Dubai were two issues that the government would want to consider together. Consequently, on the morning of 24 February, an ASIO officer took an elevator up to the office of the urbane Dennis Richardson, the secretary of the Department of Foreign Affairs. Richardson was the most senior bureaucrat reporting to Smith, so it was appropriate that ASIO first shared its news with him.

If there was anyone inside the government who could be expected to pick up on the parallels between Ben's case and the drama unfolding in Dubai, it was Richardson. Few people in Canberra had seen and done what he had. He'd been Australia's ambassador to the United States, an adviser to prime ministers, and ASIO's director-general of security. He would later become the top public servant at the Department of Defence, but in early 2010 he was one of the senior public servants responsible for Australia's overseas spies in the Australian Secret Intelligence Service.

Richardson had a reputation as a hardened spymaster, a demanding taskmaster who insisted on rigour and who was clinically efficient in dismissing those he perceived to have failed to meet standards. One source tells me he could be brutal if someone neglected to cover a possibility or was not properly prepared for a briefing. However, according to another source, 'he can be very warm and very gentle' and 'like a kindly uncle'. At ASIO he was renowned for imposing the use of the Myers–Briggs personality test on many in the agency. Richardson believed it helped people understand their own strengths and weaknesses and made them better able to work with colleagues. The test's critics deride it as shallow pop psychology, but many who were in ASIO in the early 2000s felt it helped enhance the agency's team ethos in the post-9/11 era.

Most importantly, ASIO knew that Richardson would know how to deal with the sensitive information it was delivering. Few people in government have had access to such a broad range of classified information as Richardson, and even fewer have had to analyse and parse it for political and strategic ends, and use it deftly in matters of diplomacy involving Australia's allies. Crucially, Richardson was also well versed in the imprecise language and allusions necessary for everyday bureaucracy, words that would be harmless when later dug up by internal probes.

During an inquiry three years later, Richardson would say he had 'no clear, specific recollections of the details' of Ben's arrest—apparently he wasn't even given a name.[9] But the issues that had been at stake were still clear in his mind: 'discussions in relation to the misuse of passports by Israel, and about investigations into Australians of Israeli background who may have been working for Israeli intelligence'. This could have been a reference to ASIO's tracking of Ben Zygier, or simply the Dubai passports, or both. Those who were questioning Richardson pointed out that Dubai's implications were 'a high-profile issue at the time, and a preoccupation of the national security community'.

On the same day that Richardson was briefed about Ben's arrest, another senior public servant in Smith's department, Greg Moriarty, was also told the news by ASIO. The intelligence agency clearly wanted to avoid the impression that it had tried to keep quiet about the arrest. Moriarty, a former ambassador to Iran (now the ambassador to Indonesia), was at the time responsible for intelligence matters inside the department. Unlike Richardson, Moriarty did scribble notes about the ASIO briefing in a private diary, despite being asked to make no 'formal record' of the discussion.[10] It would be because of these notes that ASIO and the Foreign Affairs Department would later argue about who should have done more to help Ben Zygier.

Moriarty wrote that he was told Ben had been arrested, that Ben worked for the Mossad, that he had access to a lawyer, that he was not being mistreated and that his family had not asked the

Australian Government for help. Importantly, Moriarty also wrote that he had spoken with the chief of staff to the Foreign Minister, Frances Adamson. She, too, was well credentialed, having formerly been Australia's deputy high commissioner to the United Kingdom. Three years later, she would tell an internal inquiry she didn't remember the conversation.

An ASIO officer also visited Attorney-General Rob McClelland's office and handed over a file on Ben Zygier. McClelland had to hand the file back after reading it, and he too was asked to make no formal record of the meeting. McClelland has never publicly detailed what he was told, but from what he said during the internal inquiry in 2013, it's clear he was given Ben's name and reminded that Ben had been under investigation by ASIO. It's also apparent that McClelland was told that ASIO would share the news about Ben with others in the Australian Government: 'I had recommended to me the course of action that ASIO proposed to take, to brief relevant agencies, departments and officials. [It was] a course of action I approved and thought was appropriate.' However, he ended up being the only minister who admitted knowing about Ben's arrest prior to 2013. No other minister seems to have been aware of Ben's fate until the ABC broadcast the story more than two years after Ben's death.

Almost twenty-four hours after the call from Dubai to Stephen Smith, a meeting of the National Security Committee of Cabinet took place, which is the closest Australia gets to the White House's situation room. While these highest-level meetings are not characterised by Hollywood's plethora of hi-tech widescreen TVs, they do allow the nation's top politicians to sit down with its spymasters, those people who have overall responsibility for intelligence and security, and access to the most secretive information available to Australian eyes. In attendance were Prime Minister Kevin Rudd, Foreign Minister Stephen Smith, the head of ASIO and other intelligence chiefs.

At this point, the media still did not know that Australian passports had been used in the Dubai assassination, but the misuse of these passports was a priority topic at the National Security Committee meeting. Less than twenty-four hours later, Rudd would publicly state that he wanted to know more about the incident: 'If Australian passports are being used or forged by any state, let alone for the purposes of assassination, this is of the deepest concern to the Australian Government.'[11] Foreign Minister Smith would echo his prime minister's comments: 'Our primary responsibility and our primary concern is the sanctity and integrity of the Australian passport.' He would say that Australian spies and officials had been 'working flat out, particularly overnight, dealing with this', contacting countries like the United Kingdom, France, Germany and Ireland 'to swap notes'. Smith would also single out McClelland as a participant in the discussions about Dubai. But there would be no mention of Ben Zygier. Smith was apparently unaware of Ben's arrest and, by implication, McClelland's direct knowledge of it.

It seems remarkable that, in spite of one federal minister—the Attorney-General—and three other high-level officials having been informed of Ben's arrest and imprisonment, this was not mentioned at the security meeting. This is especially mystifying considering the overlap between Ben's case and the passport forgeries, where the names of Melbourne-born Jews now living in Israel were appropriated by Mossad agents. How could Ben not rate a mention in the face of Prime Minister Rudd's 'deepest concern'? Yet this sentiment does not seem to have prompted either McClelland or the other officials who knew about Ben's circumstances—three former or prospective Australian ambassadors—to pass on their knowledge of the case.

It just doesn't seem plausible. ASIO seems to have acted on its recognition that the separate cases of Ben and the Dubai passports involved similar issues. Yet no-one else inside the Australian Government, including the Attorney-General, who ran ASIO, seems to have made the same connection. But it's impossible to get answers to questions about who knew what and the action the government might have taken at the time. A wall of 'national security concerns' prevents any of the participants from discussing the matter.

Some Sort of Scam

When the media finally tracked him down, the real Adam Korman, who sells and repairs musical instruments in Tel Aviv, said, 'It's identity theft, simply unbelievable. I have travelled all over the world but never visited Dubai.'[12] A neighbour agreed: 'There's no chance he is in [the] Mossad. He fixes violins.' The passport used by the Mossad agent who'd stolen Korman's name was supposedly issued on 5 November 2003 at the grand building that houses the Australian High Commission in London. Joshua Daniel Bruce's passport was supposedly issued at the same place just a day later, even though at the time, the real Joshua Daniel Bruce was in his seventh year of quietly studying his religion in Jerusalem. In Melbourne, his mother said both the date of birth and the signature on his passport were wrong. 'I am fearful, but hopefully everyone will see that it is fraud,' she said. 'It's not his photo in the pictures they're flashing around everywhere.'[13] The third misused passport originally belonged to Nicole McCabe, whose mother also lived in Melbourne. She told the media her daughter was not in the Mossad either. 'We're shocked. We don't know any more than you do,' said Jane Kramer. 'My daughter has been caught up in some sort of scam and we are very distressed.'[14]

As the Australian media raced to find and interview these passport holders, Ben's family remained in a state of fright, and his friends in a state of confusion. Ben's case was different because while the parents of the other three Australians were speaking to the media, Geoff and Louise Zygier were doing all they could not to speak to Ben's friends, let alone communicate with any journalists. Besides, in order to start looking for Ben's family, the newspapers would've needed to know what had happened to Ben.

From the moment Ben was arrested, strict Israeli laws came into force. His arrest was a state secret, as were the charges he faced. Ben was not subject to a normal court process but rather was kept under the auspices of Israel's Justice Ministry—judges had approved the way in which he was being held and ensured that his circumstances were one of Israel's best-kept secrets. It was quickly made clear to Ben and his family that any public mention of his name, the mere fact of his arrest, the allegations against him or even whom he had worked for would attract a swift and severe penalty. The implicit threat was that any such leak would rebound adversely on Ben as well.

It was this constricting silence that added to the family's pain and enhanced the confusion of those around them. The friends and relations who did press for details were effectively told not to tell anyone that Ben had disappeared. They were discouraged even from entertaining the idea of speaking to anyone not close to the family. Which is why many came to their own conclusions, in particular that Ben was hiding somewhere overseas, waiting for the repercussions of the Dubai hit to fade away because to speak out now would put him in danger.

Ben's parents were themselves finding it difficult to process what had happened. When Ben was a soldier, they'd prepared themselves for the worst sort of news. They'd contemplated hearing that he'd been injured or killed. But his imprisonment just didn't add up. Their son was an ardent Zionist who had achieved so much; all he'd ever done was work hard to prove himself to Israel. They'd been blindsided by the implications of Ben's work as a spy, and they were unable to come to grips with the import of the charges against their son—and the fact that he was being treated like a traitor.

Out of the Loop

A week after the misused Australian passports splashed into public view, Australia's security agencies were trawling for information that would complete the picture of what had happened. They'd been asked to find proof that the Mossad was behind the forgeries. The Australian Federal Police would soon be sent to Israel to listen to whatever the Israelis were willing to tell them, and to speak with the Australians whose identities had been used.

Just six months beforehand, ASIO had been following Ben and listening to his phone calls in Melbourne. Acknowledging the long-term nature of the investigation taking place, on 1 March 2010, while Ben was still in a Shin Bet interrogation cell, the organisation decided to go beyond verbally briefing those outside the agency. For the first time, it put its knowledge down on paper, combining what it knew about Ben's predicament with details of the top-of-mind issue: the Dubai passports. Ben's situation was described in neutral language, and though ASIO knew his name, the report did not mention it. The document referred to 'an unnamed dual Australian Israeli national facing charges in Israel relating to breaches of Israel's national security'.

Significantly, this submission by ASIO was sent to the office of the Prime Minister's national security adviser and that of Foreign Minister Stephen Smith's top public servant, Dennis Richardson. With the winds of the Dubai investigation sweeping through every intelligence office in Canberra, ASIO's report of Ben's arrest was also sent to the heads of all the major intelligence bodies in Australia: the Australian Secret Intelligence Service, which runs Australia's overseas spies; the Office of National Assessments, which vets intelligence for the Prime Minister; the electronic surveillance network run by what was then known as the Defence Signals Directorate (now the Australian Signals Directorate); and the body that collects and analyses information for the armed services, the Defence Intelligence Organisation.

But again, it seems no-one actually pointed out to any of the politicians (excepting the already briefed Attorney-General) that Ben was in jail. Every major intelligence agency now had on its files an instance of an Australian misusing his passport for the Mossad, yet no-one thought to tell a single minister. They were kept out of the loop.

Perhaps the bureaucrats simply assumed that if the Mossad had charged Ben, he must have done something wrong. Maybe they shared the doubts held by someone who knew Ben in the late 1990s as a university law student. 'Israel is not the sort of country that would go to such trouble to incarcerate someone for no reason,' this friend says, 'so something has gone down there. And if you look at Israel's history, every five years or so there has been a Prisoner X, so it's not that uncommon.'

With ASIO's report on his plight lying neglected on desks in Canberra, Ben was taken even deeper inside Israel's secretive prison system. For weeks he'd been held in a Shin Bet interrogation room somewhere in Tel Aviv. But once his formal questioning was over, he was sent to prison while investigators built a formal criminal case against him. On 7 March 2010, Ben was taken to the last room he would ever live in, the cell that had originally been built for Yigal Amir, the man who'd killed Yitzhak Rabin. It was not the hi-tech, suicide-proof cell it was supposed to be. It was old, its cameras needed replacing, and it was devastatingly lonely.

PRISONER X

Ayalon

When I visit Ayalon prison, it is a quiet spring evening. The sunlight is fading, bathing everything in a warm glow. Lit from behind by this comforting light, a lone guard ambles up a driveway that rises from beneath a massive wall. Judging by his light-blue shirt and the stars on his shoulders, it's likely he's a senior officer. He looks relaxed as he heads in the direction of a nearby apartment block, probably having just finished his shift. At first glance the apartments look like any other new development in Israel, uniformly white and neat, but this block looks a little desolate, separated from the nearby suburbs by the massive prison complex.

I'm not sure how long I should linger in the car park. Acting on a vague sense of paranoia, I drive off down a road that threads between the jail and a large but tatty shopping complex. I keep going until Ayalon's perimeter wall gives way to the prison service headquarters and then an ambulance station. Here, a half-dozen ambulances are lined up on a grey gravel apron beside a low-slung building, surrounded by the interlinked wire of a cyclone fence. In December 2010, one of these ambulances must have been used by the paramedics who rushed to Ben's high-security cell.

I do a U-turn and drive slowly back past the prison, watching as another guard is dropped off by his friends. Slowing almost to a stop, I see him get out of a white Mercedes with low-profile tyres. The guard slams shut the back door and then laughs as a friend flings an empty milkshake cup at him through a front window of the car. In one sweeping movement, the smiling guard scoops up the cup and flings it into a nearby bin. He lackadaisically waves goodbye to his companions, hitches his bag up on one shoulder and slouches his way towards the jail's formidable gate. A friendly exchange such as this could have taken place anywhere in Israel, but this particular man is presumably about to begin the night shift at Israel's biggest prison.

It's not much of a job, being a prison guard in Israel. A billboard just up the road from Ayalon, near the entrance to a training facility, shows a row of neatly uniformed cadets looking proud and happy. But in a country that still reserves its highest esteem for those who serve on the front line of the nation's borders, a prison guard's uniform does not carry the social cachet of an air force pilot's neatly pressed shirt, a commando's fatigues or even the plain collared shirt of a police detective or a Mossad spy. And at least some of the guards are only in the job because they have to be, doing their version of compulsory military service.

A prison is rarely a nice place to be, even if you work there. Like those involved in dreary security work all around the world, few can maintain the constant cross-checking and the filling in of logbooks in the face of the monotonous routine of prison life. When the same thing happens each day on a clockwork schedule, cutting corners and missing checklists seem inevitable. There is an inherent conundrum in this work. Constant vigilance prevents mistakes, but such vigilance is almost impossible to maintain, so systems are created to compensate for human error, or to insure against it.

Ben arrived at Ayalon on 7 March 2010, after weeks of tough interrogation. His predicament was tragically unique. Not only would he have known that he might be facing years or even decades in jail, but he was also in a special category of inmates: that reserved for Israel's most secret prisoners. There were no written orders for how he was to be treated at Ayalon, only a series of vague emails, verbal understandings and overlapping tasks. Ultimately, no-one took complete responsibility for him.

As he was brought through the jail's imposing entrance, other guards and prisoners were diverted away from him. Entering any prison is an intimidating experience, but Ben must have had an especially acute sense of foreboding as he walked down the shabby corridors. It's unlikely he was taken past the blue doors behind which lay other prisoners' cells. Most of these doors have wide grills so the prisoners can see out into the corridor, and even when the cell doors only have small slots, the prisoners can stick little hand mirrors through them to see who is approaching. But Ben was to be kept away from pretty much everyone inside the prison.

Ben's alleged crime was so significant that almost no-one on staff, from the most senior man in the prison, the deputy commissioner, down to the junior warden who brought him food, was told much about him at all—not his name, his age, what he was charged with, or how long he'd been held. Talking with him was discouraged. Ben was not even given a prisoner number. This meant that when staff wanted to communicate with each other about this inmate, rather than a shared computer file that everyone could access, these wardens relied mainly on what one guard called 'from my mouth to your ears'. Nothing was to be written down. Everything about Ben was 'in *shoo-shoo*', Hebrew slang for 'secret'. The judge who later looked into Ben's death heavily criticised this lack of detail and the compartmentalisation of information.

Ayalon doesn't have the white, clean, antiseptic feel of many of Australia's modern prisons. Its various buildings are a patchwork of different renovations and extensions, and many of the corridors are scarred by the repeated passage of food trolleys. Behind the heavy chain mail on the regular cells' external windows, the bunks are basic, made of square metal tubing and chipboard, and there are simple plastic moulded chairs. Many of the prisoners personalise their cells a little with posters and photos from home. While circulating in the prison, most of the population wears a highly visible orange uniform made from a similar canvas as a tradesman's tough work clothes, with a white singlet or T-shirt underneath. In their cells, however, many of the prisoners wear whatever clothes they like.

From his first day at Ayalon, Ben also dressed as he wished. But his cell was different from any other and lay deep within the prison. To get there, guards followed a corridor that ran from the command centre past the most secure wing of the prison, on the southern side of the complex. The cell was built here so that other inmates would rarely walk past it. It was described by the guards as a 'realm within a realm'. Cell 15, which was Ben's, and the adjacent cell 13—whose existence would come as a surprise during my research—could only be approached via a guardroom. Wardens would sit in this room and check out visitors as they arrived, as well as watching several monitors connected to the closed-circuit cameras inside the two cells. They would communicate with Ben using a basic intercom— unlike other cell doors, Ben's had no grill or slot. The first time they closed that door on him, it must have been one of the lowest moments of his life.

For most of every day, Ben was completely alone. But even though he was a high-security prisoner, he could make telephone calls from his cell. A prison insider tells me Ben had 'a regular phone in the cell' and could use it whenever he wanted, though he could only call 'specific people' and all of the exchanges were monitored. During the months of his imprisonment, he would regularly call his lawyer, his mother and his wife. Ben also had his own bathroom, connected to his cell by a transparent door.

The part of Ayalon prison in which Ben was kept has a long history of housing Israel's very worst criminals. Besides Yigal Amir, previous inmates of the block include notorious gangsters like

Francois 'the Great' Abutbul, who was kept in this cell so he couldn't be harmed by rival criminal gangs. Nothing happened to him at Ayalon, but less than a year after being released, Abutbul was killed by two motorcycle-riding gunmen. Another infamous prisoner was Adolf Eichmann, one of the last surviving key figures of the Nazi regime. He was kidnapped in Argentina by a team of Mossad agents who brought him to Israel to stand trial for war crimes. One of the best-known pictures of Eichmann shows him near one of Ayalon's high stone walls, pacing past a chair. He was hanged on the grounds of the prison in 1962.

Eichmann and Amir are more than notorious in Israel. Their actions made them intensely despised. So jailing Ben in the same place they were jailed sent the heaviest of messages. It was a brutal punishment, albeit one that many inside the Mossad and Shin Bet probably felt he deserved. The two agencies are the guardians of Israel's most critical secrets, and Ben had been accused of spilling at least one—related to operations against Iran—into the outside world. He had breached the crucial article of faith that governs every intelligence agency: secrets must remain secret. And so Ben was held under the tightest security that Israel could muster. But it was security that compromised his rights and his care.

In Distress

On Ben's first day in Ayalon, he spoke to a social worker, 'Julia'. Terrified at finding himself alone in a prison cell, he told Julia that he was having suicidal thoughts. The social worker took Ben through a 'suicide forecast' test. The results were alarming, but there was no psychiatrist on stand-by at the prison to deal with the situation. Normally, when a prisoner is brought into the maximum-security prison, their first day includes an assessment by an official committee made up of a doctor, a psychiatrist and a social worker. It is a stringent part of Israel's prison service procedure. But it wasn't followed in Ben's case because of the secrecy imposed by the intelligence agencies. In fact, the many Israeli court documents that were released over the course of 2013 showed that there were very few regulations that applied to Ben. And without rules, in a place as highly ordered and bureaucratised as a prison, any system is more likely to fail.

Julia was worried enough by what Ben told her that she did not wait for a regular prison service psychiatrist to arrive, which could have taken days. In nearly five weeks of Ben being interrogated and held under lock and key, this woman was the first person who made his needs a priority. She immediately called in an external psychiatrist, asking him to come to the prison that evening. The interview with the psychiatrist was thorough and Ben's trauma was evident. The psychiatrist recommended the use of sleeping tablets and tranquilisers to calm Ben down. But he noted that 'there was no suicidal risk'. Right up until a few hours before Ben's death nine months later, his calm exterior would confound many other doctors, social workers, psychiatrists, even his lawyers. Tragically, only his mother would raise the alarm when Ben's despair was seemingly at its peak.

Later on that first day, Ben also met the man who would exert more power over his life in prison than anyone else. Of all the people in Ayalon, Intelligence Officer Ofer knew the most about Ben. According to court documents, Deputy Commissioner Amar, who ran the prison, said, 'Everything goes through him [Ofer]. He is the only person taking care of Ben.' Every aspect of Ben's life in Ayalon had a security angle, and it was either approved or denied by Ofer. It was his job to ensure that not one skerrick of information that Ben had gathered as a Mossad agent was leaked to his wife or lawyer or anyone else. So he approved visits from legal advisers and family, supervised the medical care, coordinated regular meetings with psychiatrists, regulated Ben's meals and monitored the food in his fridge, and cast an ear towards every phone call Ben made or received.

Ofer was employed by the prison service, but inside the walls of Ayalon he was more like a proxy for the Mossad and Shin Bet. He represented the blurred lines of responsibility that helped decide

Ben's fate. Ofer was the personification of a two-pronged failure: spies had outsourced the jailing of Ben Zygier, and the prison service had ceded responsibility for Ben to the spooks outside the prison walls. In effect, no-one was in control, certainly not the deputy commissioner, who testified that 'cell 15 did not exist from my point of view'.

According to court documents, on day one of Ben's imprisonment, Ofer sent an email to the two most senior people in the prison, Deputy Commissioner Amar and the facility's operating officer, specifying that Ben was to be held in isolation and describing him as an inmate 'in distress [and to be] under supervision 24 hours a day'. What 'distress' meant and what sort of supervision it merited were not spelt out. There were no instructions that flowed from this to Ben's wardens. The email wasn't even printed out and filed, nor was it made accessible in Ayalon's computer system. It just seems to have faded into the digital distance.

On Ben's second day in prison, Julia and the external psychiatrist attempted to determine what sort of supervision would help prevent Ben from hurting himself. They decided that he should be placed at the bottom of the scale used to categorise distressed inmates.

Prisoners defined as Level A-plus suffer from extreme psychological distress and are at the highest possible risk of committing suicide. These prisoners are often shifted to what the guards call 'spaceships', cells measuring roughly 6 metres by 3 metres that have bare walls, a thin blue mattress, a stainless-steel squat toilet and CCTV cameras high up in the ceiling. Inmates are only supposed to be kept in these cells for a few days at a time. One step down the self-harm scale are the prisoners assessed at Level A. They are thought to have a high risk of suicide and are also supposed to be constantly monitored in their cells, as was the case with Yigal Amir—for some months while he was in cell 15, guards sat and watched him for every minute of every hour he was there.

Yet another step down the scale is Level B. These inmates are in psychological distress and there is the possibility of self-harm, but they are not deemed 'high risk'. This was the level recommended for Ben. According to prison rules, these inmates can be held in a regular cell, but wherever possible the prisoner should not be left alone. Also, any inmate subject to any of these three ratings is supposed to have their cell regularly searched for any object that may be hidden and later used as an instrument of self-harm. As a result, Julia told Ben's wardens that he had to be checked every half-hour using the cameras inside his cell. When this check had been done, it was supposed to be recorded in the logbook that was kept in the guardroom outside Ben's cell. The guards also had to check that the cameras in Ben's cell were working properly, day and night.

The problem with all this is that prison orders, like any instructions given in a highly structured place, are only the beginning of a routine. They need to be cross-checked by superior officers to ensure they are carried out. Every other routine in the prison had a chain of command and a hierarchy of responsibility, backed up by a centralised computer file with boxes that needed to be ticked. But maintaining a system of monitoring for the mystery prisoner in cell 15 was more a matter of general understanding than strict obligation for the guards involved. This was compounded by the commander of the prison being told to butt out of anything to do with Ben's security or welfare—Intelligence Officer Ofer, while he was more junior, was 'taking care of the prisoner from A to Z'.

Equally damaging were the constraints placed on what Ben could say to anyone. The people he saw most often were the lower-ranked guards, yet they knew the least about him, not even his name, and he was discouraged from speaking with them. Julia and her later replacement Leila at least knew his name and the basic fact that he'd been accused of breaching national security. But neither of these social workers knew the full details of Ben's alleged crimes, nor did the many psychiatrists he saw. Ben could not speak frankly with those who were chiefly responsible for his mental health about what he'd been charged with or his work with the Mossad. It limited his ability to discuss his torment with them. Maybe this was why it would take him so long to tell a psychiatrist that he'd previously attempted suicide. Ben could talk in depth with his lawyers, but they weren't qualified to look after his mental and emotional wellbeing. And in these conversations he displayed a certain detachment, an almost professional air that only served to hide any signs of distress.

So the guards who knew Ben the least saw him the most, the social workers who were most able to help him were handicapped by what they didn't know, and the lawyers who knew the most about his situation were not qualified to care for him. In terms of mental disintegration, it was a perfect storm.

At the end of April, Ben's frame of mind began spiralling downwards. He'd seen a psychiatrist on the evening he'd arrived at the prison, at the start of March, and again a week later. But then six weeks had passed before he saw a psychiatrist again. In May, the reality of Ben's situation must have really begun to set in. The birth of his second child was two months away, and Ben would have feared never seeing that child outside prison, confronted by the prospect of decades spent living alone in a jail cell. Ben began to ask repeatedly for help from a psychiatrist.

Meanwhile, in Raanana, where her neighbours simply assumed she was a single mother, Haya was worried about her calls and emails being monitored. She was also stressed about devising a cover story for Ben's disappearance. By now, some of his friends in Israel knew that he was in trouble, but not that he was in jail. Most of his friends in Australia, however, were not even aware that Ben had run afoul of his employer. Many simply assumed his covert work had stepped up a notch, putting him out of contact for important operational reasons.

According to one of her neighbours, during this time Haya was a little aloof but seemingly at peace. 'Haya acted normally, like any mother,' says the neighbour, adding, 'She's very beautiful.' Some who saw her every day even claimed they were told that her husband had been diagnosed with cancer and had returned to Australia for treatment.

Back in Ayalon, Ben's request was granted and he saw a psychiatrist five times in the six-week period between the end of

April and the beginning of June. The voluminous court documents dealing with Ben's death don't clearly state what drove these repeated visits. But it was around that time that Ben's assigned social worker, Julia, was replaced by another prison service social worker, Leila, and this swap might have unsettled Ben. Like Julia, Leila also grew concerned about Ben's mental state, meeting with him at least once a week, but she had no opportunity to discuss her alarm with her superior officers or other mental health professionals.

According to the judge who investigated Ben's death, during one of Julia's final meetings with Ben, in May, 'she noticed a superficial cut on his arm ... He told her he did it because of the pressure he was under, and in order to calm down.' Ben apparently then denied having suicidal intentions, and even claimed he'd cut himself just because he was bored. Perhaps this incident should have rung alarm bells. Ben had hurt himself while undergoing intensive psychiatric care and while he was supposedly being monitored by cameras every half-hour, using an implement that had obviously not been found during one of the regular searches of his cell. Yet there was no reassessment of the need to keep a closer eye on the mystery prisoner.

The prison guards also often saw Ben weeping in his cell, especially after a visit from his family, and they would call the social worker to let her know. But it seems it was such a regular occurrence that they simply let Ben calm himself down, sometimes with television, at other times with the tranquilisers and sleeping pills that he was prescribed.

Kicking up a Fuss

Fifty-two days after Ben was arrested, on the afternoon of 23 March 2010, British Foreign Secretary David Miliband rose to his feet in the House of Commons. He wanted to express his government's 'deep unhappiness' at what he described as the 'cloning and counterfeiting' of British passports. He also wanted to announce radical action: the United Kingdom was going to expel the Mossad's station chief from London.

The British equivalent of the FBI, the Serious Organised Crime Agency, had spent the past month investigating where the British passports used in the Dubai hit had come from. It discovered that the twelve people whose identities were said to have been used by the Mossad were either Jewish visitors to Israel or people who had taken up residence there. The conclusion reached by the British investigators was stark and simple: the only link between all the fake passports was travel in and out of Israel, especially via Tel Aviv's Ben Gurion Airport. It seemed that after the passport bearers had innocently handed over the documents, the data had been copied, stored and then passed on to the Mossad. And the forgeries were clearly part of a long-term operation, because one of the passports had been cloned two years before the Dubai operation.

When you arrive at Ben Gurion Airport, you descend a massive, wide ramp that feeds passengers from the arrival lounges into the passport queue. It takes a good few minutes to negotiate this ramp, and as you do so, you look up at massive sandstone tableaus of biblical scenes that are meant to evoke tours of Israel's historical sites. The passport check itself is usually routine and can involve a young security official asking numerous detailed questions: Who are you visiting? How do you know them? Where will you stay? Why are you here? Where did you study? Where else have you travelled? What do you know about Israel? If you are Jewish, the questions extend to which youth movement you participated in, which synagogue you attended, and whether you've been to Israel before. If there is a stamp in your passport from certain other countries in the Middle East, the questioning can be much more intensive and intrusive, as Israel takes its airport security extremely seriously. And sometimes, your passport is borrowed by one of the young officials, who wanders away to query a superior. The British claim shone a new light on the experience of having your passport taken not only out of your hands, but also out of your sight.

When I landed in Israel in 2006 to report on the impending national election, I had my passport taken from me. I waited in a small office, barred from entering the main arrivals hall, while someone, somewhere, checked some detail of my passport. I was not told what the issue was—no-one explained to me why this detention was necessary. At first I was simply bewildered, then I became frustrated, then I got angry. I was forced to wait more than six hours, without explanation. When my passport was finally returned to me, my queries were answered with a bored shrug of the official's shoulders. The message in that shrug was clear: if I demanded to know why the passport had been examined, I would have to wait even longer to get out of the airport.

The British investigation was the first by any security body to officially and publicly claim that Israel used border checks like this to help acquire passports for its intelligence agencies. But then, the United Kingdom had had similar issues with Israel in the past. It knew when to keep quiet, and when to kick up a fuss.

Back in 1986, eight British passports were found in a telephone booth in West Germany. They had been left there inadvertently, in an envelope bearing the mark of the Israeli embassy in London, and they were very good forgeries. Britain's main intelligence agency, MI6, was furious and demanded a response from Tel Aviv, but that was slow in coming. Then, the following year in London, two Palestinians who were double agents for the Mossad assisted in the shooting of a Palestinian cartoonist targeted by the Palestine Liberation Organization. While it was not a Mossad operation, the Israelis knew about the hit in advance and had not stopped it from going ahead. Then Prime Minister Margaret Thatcher was furious and shut down the Mossad's station in the United Kingdom, expelling the facility's chief for 'activities incompatible with his status'. In response, the Mossad moved its station to Brussels.

It took years for the agency to formally return to London, and it only happened after a formal agreement was reached between the Mossad and Britain's intelligence services, which involved an explicit undertaking given by Israel's then Foreign Minister Shimon Peres. In the wake of the Dubai controversy in 2010, Miliband would not confirm what that agreement had entailed. But the Mossad station chief in London was again expelled. The banishment only lasted until the end of the year, however, when the relationship between the United Kingdom and Israel was repaired. In December, around the time of Ben Zygier's death, the outgoing Mossad chief, Meir Dagan, travelled to London with the man who would replace him, Tamir Pardo, introducing him to the heads of MI5 and MI6.[1]

There was also retaliation from each of the other countries whose passports were abused by the Mossad in Dubai, though this diplomatic dance looked a little bit too ritualistic, a habitual pro-forma protest made without any real expectation of change by Israel. In June 2010, Ireland expelled a Mossad agent from the Israeli embassy in Dublin. In Germany, it was a little more embarrassing for Israel because the police issued an arrest warrant for an agent who'd helped obtain the one genuine German passport, and he was finally detained in Warsaw. Like the agents convicted in New Zealand, Uri Brodsky ended up facing the possibility of a trial— the image of a Mossad agent scurrying away while trying to hide his face from the media was also reminiscent of the awkwardness in Auckland. But Brodsky was allowed to return to Israel while on bail. A few months later he was charged by German authorities with more serious offences, but this merely ensured the agent would never return to the country.

Like the United Kingdom, Ireland and Germany later resumed normal relations with Israel. In Australia, however, the aftermath of the reaction to what happened in Dubai was a little different. The use of Australian passports in the emirate, and the handling of Ben Zygier's case, both seem to have left their mark on relations between Canberra and Tel Aviv.

In the first half of 2010, ASIO and the Mossad began one of the rockiest chapters in their mutual history. In the weeks after the revelations about Dubai, there was almost no communication between Tel Aviv and Canberra. This was the case even though the Australian Federal Police had been dispatched to Israel, which was a real measure of the Australian Government's displeasure. According to a US diplomatic cable published by WikiLeaks, Australian officials were "'furious" all the way up the chain of command over the incident'. By May, ASIO boss David Irvine had also landed in Tel Aviv as part of Canberra's effort to get the Mossad to tell them more. The Australian Government has since said that Irvine did not raise Ben's incarceration while he was in Israel, and it seems he wasn't given much new information about the Dubai passports either.

Foreign Minister Stephen Smith carried out Australia's official retribution on 24 May, announcing the expulsion of the Mossad's man in Canberra. The sting in the tail was the revelation of much that is usually kept quiet. For the first time, an Australian Government minister directly accused the Mossad of cloning its passports. But Smith went further, stating publicly that the Mossad had a history of using counterfeit Australian passports in its foreign operations. 'Our passports have previously been misused by Israel,' Smith told a TV interviewer. 'As a consequence of that, there was an understanding between Australia and Israel that it would not happen again. That's been broken.'[2] Smith went on to reveal that the previous forgeries had taken place before 2007, something that had never been reported, let alone spoken about by a government minister.

Smith was more circumspect when he talked about the expelled Mossad man. He was careful not to use the words 'intelligence agency' or spell out the man's position at the Israeli embassy. 'In accordance with the usual diplomatic traditions, I'm not proposing to identify that particular person,' said Smith, adding only that there was a parallel with the action taken in the United Kingdom.

While the Foreign Minister was taking a stand on the passports issue, Ben Zygier still did not seem to be on Smith's radar—this despite an ASIO report detailing how an Australian was in jail in Israel on serious espionage charges, a man with a history of misusing his Australian passport. And given what Ben had done in Europe, a close reading of the following comments by Smith raises more questions: 'We believe it is in our national interest and Israel's national interest for there to be cooperation ... in the challenges that confront not just Israel, not just the Middle East, but the international community; for example, Iran's nuclear program.' With the Mossad likely speculating that ASIO may have leaked the nature of Ben's work, this statement would have raised eyebrows in Israel. Such speculation could have been prompted by the phone calls Ben had received from Jason Koutsoukis, or by the journalist's story—published earlier that year—about three unnamed Australian men using their passports for Mossad work.

Stephen Smith's strong condemnation of the Mossad, a lead that Ireland and Germany would soon follow, was criticised by Australia's Liberal–National Coalition. The Opposition said Israel had been dealt with harshly and insisted that the Rudd government had gone too far. First, it pointed out minor details that had apparently annoyed the Israelis, such as TV news cameras being strategically positioned to capture the Israeli ambassador on his way to hear the official Australian protest. More importantly, the Australian Government had then revealed the name of the expelled Mossad officer. When an updated list of the diplomats assigned to Canberra's embassies was released, the Mossad officer's name was given as one of two counsellors at the Israeli embassy, and he was the only one to have recently departed. The Mossad had immediately assumed the name had been deliberately released, but the government insisted it was an accident.

Shadow Foreign Affairs Minister Julie Bishop questioned why a serious response like an expulsion from an embassy was necessary when it received little coverage in the Israeli media. But while highlighting this, she made headline news of her own in Israel. In an interview with the Fairfax press, she made an admission that politicians are not supposed to make, one that was particularly damaging because it came from someone who aspired to be Australia's foreign minister. 'It would be naive to think Israel is the only country in the world that has used forged passports,' said Bishop, staring at the camera as if considering whether she should continue. 'There are many things that governments do, including Australia, in operations with other countries that would include the use of passports.'[3] Though she would later try to deny she'd uttered these words, she'd admitted that Australia forges passports for its spies too.

It was classic 'gotcha' journalism, which made news in Australia as well as Israel, and sparked a debate about politicians not being able to state the obvious. But it helped mask an increasing deterioration of the relations between Israel and Australia. And in hindsight, it also hid what seems to be a remarkable failure of the Australian Government: Why did no-one connect this Australia–Israel crisis with Ben Zygier's plight?

No Recollection

By mid-2010, many different parts of the Australian intelligence bureaucracy knew that Ben was in prison in Israel. Two separate ASIO reports containing references to Ben's situation had been circulated to the major intelligence agencies and the offices of ministers and senior public servants. But the predicament facing the Australian citizen deep inside Ayalon had not been relayed to any ministers. Even Attorney-General Robert McClelland had not once raised Ben's jailing when discussing Dubai with his peers. This apparent lack of communication later greatly embarrassed the Australian Government.

When Ben's story finally came to light in February 2013 on the ABC's *Foreign Correspondent* program, Foreign Minister Bob Carr featured in the report. He said, on camera, that his department only found out about Ben's case when his body was brought back to Australia in December 2010. Carr was subsequently furious that he had been given the wrong information, and he demanded answers. The Department of Foreign Affairs initiated an inquiry to track down which pieces of information were sent to which ministers' offices. And for the first time, someone publicly doubted the government's claim that it had missed the connection between Ben's plight and the saga in Dubai.

The Opposition's Julie Bishop said that some of those who were cooperating with the internal inquiry could be concealing what they knew:

At the very same time [Ben's] matter arose, the Government was in the process of expelling a Mossad agent from Australia. That's why I'm so concerned as to why this didn't ring alarm bells anywhere in the government, even though the highest levels of government were aware that an Australian citizen had been detained ... and he had a number of passports.[4]

Bishop seized on the fact that the people who did know about Ben's incarceration in 2010 had then been working for the Foreign Minister and were now ambassadors to China and Indonesia. She said the recollections of Stephen Smith were simply not believable: 'Stephen Smith is yet to give any explanation as to how it is he didn't see the written briefings nor receive the briefings.' Kevin Rudd, who was prime minister at the time, had also claimed he was never told of Ben's situation, an assertion that Bishop derided: 'Interestingly, this was at the very time that the Australian Government was in a lather about Australian passports being used by Israeli intelligence agencies. So somebody must have thought maybe there was a connection, maybe there are questions to ask.'[5]

Three years after the event, journalists were incredulous at the account of the National Security Committee of Cabinet meeting in February 2010, as Bob Carr discovered when—his own disbelief obvious on his face—he addressed an astonished bunch of journalists in the media briefing room at Parliament House:

REPORTER: The Dubai police chief rings up Australia and says Australian passports were used in an assassination in Dubai and an Australian national is arrested in Israel, [and] that information was never passed on to the relevant ministers?

BOB CARR: No, it wasn't.

REPORTER: What do you think of that?

BOB CARR: Well, I can't pretend it's satisfactory.

REPORTER: Do you find it extraordinary that this report says the then foreign minister has no recollection of the Zygier case during his time as foreign minister, and the then head of DFAT, Mr Richardson, has no recollection?

BOB CARR: No, I don't, because this is a consular case—it's a story of someone who has got Israeli citizenship dying in Israel. It was not considered significant at the time.

REPORTER: Despite our intelligence services being told on the same day he was arrested …

BOB CARR: Listen pal, I wasn't in the parliament at that time. I can't shed any more light on it.[6]

There are crucial questions about what was going on inside the Australian Government in 2010 for which I can get no answers. Ben's arrest and the Mossad's Dubai hit have significant parallels—both involved the Mossad using Australian passports, both involved Jews born in Melbourne who'd moved to Israel, both involved the Mossad ignoring previous arrangements with Australia, and both involved ASIO investigating exactly how Australia's passports had been misused. I tried repeatedly to speak with Bob Carr and Julie Bishop, with no success. Robert McClelland doesn't return several phone messages and emails. In fact, no government minister who was in the National Security Committee of Cabinet in 2010 has ever publicly answered any questions about this issue. ASIO doesn't respond to my questions either.

Without any official denial or confirmation, it's still an open question whether ASIO leaked Ben's identity and his work to a journalist. Jason Koutsoukis insists his source was inside Australian intelligence, and I believe him. An Australian national security source suggests to me the alternative scenario that Ben most likely provided information to Koutsoukis. But this makes no sense to me, and it's a suggestion that is publicly dismissed by Israel. In 2013, one of the statements released by the office of the Israeli leader, Benjamin Netanyahu, reads: 'The Prime Minister's office stresses that the late Mr. Zygier had no contact with the Australian security agencies.' The office also claimed there was no bad blood between the two countries, that Israeli and Australian security agencies enjoyed 'excellent cooperation' and had 'full coordination and complete transparency in dealing with current issues'. But compared with the relations between Tel Aviv and the European countries drawn into the Dubai saga, a somewhat larger scar still blights Canberra's association with Israel.

Even before the Dubai hit, the Mossad had been thinking about getting out of Canberra, shifting its resources to Asia. But still, it had not appreciated being kicked out in 2010. By then, the Mossad had also been contemplating who had blown Ben's cover. He'd told his interrogators about the calls from Koutsoukis, and while ASIO had been a possible source of the leaking of Ben's name, the 'accidental' revelation of the expelled Israeli diplomat's name raised the possibility that the Australian Government was aggressively pursuing the Mossad. The agency has since opened up an office in Seoul, where it probably feels it has more to gain by watching developments in North Korea and China.[7] The ill feeling between Israel and Australia continues to fester—at the time of writing, the Mossad still hasn't sent a publicly acknowledged officer back to Canberra.

The Man without a Name

'Nobody knows who he is and what charges he is being jailed for,' read the story that popped up on a popular Israeli website in June 2010, soon after the Israeli diplomat was expelled from Canberra. It contained startling claims from an anonymous prison service official: 'Nobody talks to him, nobody sees him, nobody visits him, nobody knows he is in jail.'

A lot had been going on in Ben's life that month, including the discovery that he'd cut his own arm. It's possible that because this wasn't acted on inside Ayalon prison, somebody risked the wrath of the law and sent a message out to the media. Whoever it was faced jail if it could be proved they'd leaked Ben's story.

The report disappeared from the website *Y-Net* almost as soon as it was posted, a casualty of Israel's military censors—the country's media are constrained by strong legal rulings that ban the publication of stories seen to run counter to Israel's national interest. But before the story vanished, some bloggers and journalists interested in security issues had noticed this first mention of a mysterious Prisoner X. Some of them sought authorisation to investigate and write more.

One such reporter, Yossi Melman, who was working at the time for the newspaper *Ha'aretz*, went to court in Petach Tikva just east of Tel Aviv to seek permission to report on Prisoner X. On that sunny, humid afternoon, Melman sat on the plaintiff's bench in the court of Judge Hila Gerstel, opposite his lawyer and the lawyers for Israel's security establishment. He was hoping to get some of the Prisoner X story on the public record. 'I didn't know his name,' Melman tells me, '[but] I assumed he was a Mossad guy and that he had done something that violated something—the organisation, its code or the law.' Then Melman says tersely, 'We lost the case. I wonder what would have happened had the judge given her consent. Would that have prevented Ben Zygier from committing suicide?'

Melman is a veteran journalist and author, with decades of experience reporting on Israel's intelligence agencies. He can be a whirlwind of energy, opinions and obscure facts. 'You make your argument and then you have to leave the court,' Melman says to me ruefully. 'And then the security services speak to the judge in private—you wait outside—and they show the judge so-called secret information. And you don't know what the secret material is.' Based on previous experiences, he had expected to lose the case. But he says that the Mossad was stupid in ignoring what would happen when the story was finally exposed. 'Okay, they managed to contain the information, to keep the information in Israel for a while,' he says, 'but they made a big mistake.'

From the initial *Y-Net* story in 2010 to the ABC's major revelation concerning Ben's identity in early 2013, several details reported by journalists were wrong. The Israeli and Australian public were better informed because of these efforts, but allegations such as the claim that Ben was not allowed any visitors helped fuel the outrage when the story finally exploded in the global media. Melman believes the Mossad could have contained that damage by releasing a few crucial details, such as how many times Ben had been visited by lawyers, social workers and family members.

Inside Ayalon prison, Ben may have heard that his story had been mentioned on the internet, but it is unlikely because this didn't receive much coverage at the time—no other Israeli media were game enough to brave the censors and repeat the story. Instead, the pain of his days in jail would have been growing. Then, in July, Ben became a father again. It must have lifted his spirits, because after multiple visits from a psychiatrist in May, there's no indication from his prison records that he saw a psychiatrist again until the beginning of August.

I'm told that Haya visited the prison with their newborn daughter soon after the birth. The strain on her would have been immense. She'd had to go through this second birth while helping her husband coordinate his legal fight, at the same time pretending in the company of most of her friends that everything was normal. What should have been one of the most joyful moments in Ben and Haya's lives couldn't even be properly shared with those closest to them. Friends of Haya's in Israel knew what was going on, but some of the people Ben knew best in Melbourne were simply left to assume that Ben was enjoying the happy occasion. One friend says that when Haya posted photos of the baby on Facebook, she didn't even ask where Ben was: 'I just thought Ben was taking the photos.'

Whoever had leaked Ben's story to *Y-Net* was far better informed than most of Ben's friends. One quote in the story, from a prison official, reflected much of the mystery of Ben's existence and showed that at least some within Israel's justice system were uncomfortable with the manner in which he was being held:

> He is simply a person without a name and without an identity who was placed in complete and absolute isolation from the outside world. I doubt even the jailers in charge of him know who he is. There is too much confidentiality surrounding him. It is scary that in 2010 a man is imprisoned in Israel without us even knowing who he is.

Some people actually knew everything about Ben. They included the judges who'd agreed to start hearing his case. They were working under the auspices of Israel's Justice Ministry, but this would be no regular trial. In fact, it would barely be a trial at all.

I try several times by phone to leave a request to speak with some of these judges, but I have no success. That leaves me standing by a graffiti-covered door in a run-down part of Tel Aviv. It's just a short drive from here to the office block where Ben once worked, but that corporate legal realm feels like it's a world away from this place. Sweat runs down my back beneath my shirt as I struggle to work the faulty intercom and explain that I am here to see the prominent human rights lawyer Michael Sfard. As my Hebrew falters, next door at the low-price fruit-juice stall, two older men suck on their cigarettes and sit lazily in wicker chairs, alternately watching me and their prospective customers slowly walk by in the hot sun.

After being admitted through the heavy security door and walking up a flight of stairs, I enter a series of book-lined offices filled with tastefully old second-hand wooden furniture, potted palms and the hum of activists busily working against what they see as the oppressive forces of the state. Sfard is most angry with the judges who agreed to hear Ben's case. Sitting in his cool office with a cup of tea nestled in his hands, the activist lawyer casually explains the principled objection he had to Ben's treatment. He says even though three district court judges agreed to participate in

Ben's case, the whole process was conducted outside of the normal Israeli judicial system. Many Israelis would accept such conditions under assurances that it was done for reasons of national security. But some, like Sfard, are disturbed that the judges even decided to accept the case. He says that judges are the only ones who are truly independent and free, and that judges thereby have the 'legal legitimacy, [the] public legitimacy to say, "[These are] our red lines. And in a democratic country, we will not take part in a secret trial."' However, Sfard knows he is in the minority, that the legal instincts of the judges are mirrored by those of most Israelis.

I suggest to Sfard that most of his fellow citizens trust the authorities to only keep secrets if there is a good enough reason. 'The Israeli public is ready to sacrifice human rights ... when it comes to national security,' he responds, adding that they do not understand 'the ramifications of such a concession, and how it can come back and haunt them'.

His Final Secret

As 2010 wore on, more and more of Ben's friends in Melbourne realised something was terribly wrong. It wasn't only that Ben had been out of contact for quite a long time. His parents, Geoff and Louise, had withdrawn from their usually busy roles within the Jewish community. They barely saw anyone, and when they did appear, they looked grey and thin and were sometimes barely able to talk beyond basic pleasantries. The pain on their faces was clear, and many felt they could not ask about the mystery of their son's plight.

Inside Ayalon prison, Ben continued to see his lawyers regularly as well as his social worker, Leila. He also saw a psychiatrist once a month between August and October. A small courtyard was connected to Ben's cell where he would pace up and down surrounded by tall, metal-covered walls, something he probably did often over these months as the weather was still warm. But it was a squashed, brutal, isolated version of the outside world. Ben could see the sky from his private yard, but the view was obscured by security netting, and the door leading outside from his cell locked automatically at night. In this yard, Ben remained isolated from human contact, unseen by any other prisoner, reflecting the situation inside his cell.

After the tough time Ben had suffered through in May, he seemed to have coped pretty well with being locked up in prison while his second daughter was born. But in November he plunged into a profound personal crisis. He and Haya had been struggling to maintain their relationship amid the strain of separation and the pressure of keeping his situation secret. Haya's prison visits were difficult for both of them, and among their close circle of family and friends, some feared that the marriage could not withstand Ben's long-term incarceration.

The family birthdays that Ben was missing added a new level of emotional stress. Just twelve months earlier, he'd been together with his family and friends in his parents' home in Melbourne, with a new future about to unfold. Now he was stuck in prison while his eldest daughter celebrated her third birthday, and in Melbourne his younger sister was turning thirty. Louise had taken her daughter out for her birthday, and they'd planned a party. The daughter, seeing that her parents were struggling to cope, asked her uncle Willy and aunt Deborah to sing for her family and friends on her birthday. It was a rare moment of celebration in a year that had felt desperately sad for the Zygier family.

It wasn't only missing such key milestones that hurt Ben so deeply. His was a family that had once delighted others with the joy they'd displayed when together, and they had usually spoken with each other several times a day. Now Ben faced unknown years on the other side of the world, restricted even in how much he could see his own children.

Unsurprisingly, he saw a psychiatrist twice in November. He was falling apart, and his final secret, which he'd managed to keep hidden despite the pressures of jail, could no longer be kept. After nine months in custody, he finally admitted that he'd previously tried to take his own life. The revelation raises a host of questions about why the prison psychiatrists had failed to uncover such a vital piece of information in Ben's previous months in Ayalon. Perhaps the signs were too difficult to pick up, though this seems unlikely. In the years before Ben went to prison, his friends had recognised a growing fragility. They'd noticed his sudden mood changes and his issues with food—some were even aware that he'd previously deliberately hurt himself. Remarkably, Ben's admission didn't prompt a reassessment by his psychiatrist or social worker of how closely he should be watched by his guards.

At the end of November, soon after this important confession, Ben was examined by a medical doctor who found a small lump in his chest, prompting concern that it could be a form of breast cancer. The doctor was also worried about Ben's mental state. Court documents revealed that she 'sensed that he could harm himself and shared her impression with security officials'. But despite the doctor's warning, it was another five days before Ben was again visited by a psychiatrist. After this meeting, the psychiatrist expressed her own concerns about Ben's admission that he was not swallowing the tranquilisers and other medication he'd been given. The implications were clear: he could have been stockpiling the pills in preparation for a suicide attempt. Once again, this valid worry was dismissed because the guards said they had seen Ben tilting his head back and swallowing the pills on the fuzzy images transmitted by the surveillance cameras in his cell. They also had never found a hidden store of pills.

At Ben's final psychiatric examination on 5 December, the clinician, who specialised in prison inmates, judged that Ben was 'without any change or fear of suicidal tendencies or psychological distress'. The psychiatrist's assessment was that there had been no change in Ben's anxiety levels and that his behaviour was not abnormal. This evaluation was backed up by the social worker, who wrote a similar report a few days later.

And so, despite Ben's desperate condition and his declaration of past suicide attempts, he remained subject to the same level of monitoring as on the day he'd entered the prison. Ben's family and wife knew of Ben's previous attempts to kill himself, but perhaps, given the evaluation by the psychiatrist in November, they assumed that because he was receiving psychological care, he'd already revealed all that had happened.

It seems reasonable to conclude that the secrecy surrounding Ben's detention did not encourage the proper monitoring of his welfare. The prison officials merely hosted the inmate; they didn't control his care. The spy agencies simply gave advice on security, so they weren't accountable for Ben's psychological health either. And the fact that the casual division of responsibility between the agencies and the prison was never detailed meant that each could repudiate their formal responsibilities. This utterly confused duty of care is the crux of why no-one was watching when Ben died.

Uncomfortable Theories

On 13 December, two days before Ben's death, a lumbering, brooding lawyer named Avigdor Feldman turned up at the massive blue-and-white entrance to Ayalon prison. One of Israel's best-known civil rights lawyers, Feldman is often seen on Israeli television screens when activists challenge the limits of the national security establishment. As he passed through the prison's security, Feldman was being scrutinised by video. He was being observed by the handful of officers in the prison's command centre, which is embedded within the white, multi-storey building that sits within Ayalon's imposing walls. These officers electronically monitor everything that happens throughout the complex, scanning wide-screen televisions that accept the feeds from 300 cameras around the prison—or at least, that's supposed to be the idea. They watched as Feldman was ushered down various corridors, past the isolated guardroom and into Ben's cell. They kept watching as Feldman, the serial defender of those who've run afoul of Israel's intelligence agencies, sat and talked with his new client. Feldman had been brought in to give Ben a second legal opinion. Ben and his family were thinking of changing their legal strategy, wondering if they should more forcefully challenge the Israeli system that seemed bent on locking their son in jail for years and perhaps decades. They wanted to ask if he should consider the plea bargain he was being offered by prosecutors.

'He seemed rational and focused,' Feldman told Israeli radio, 'but don't get the sense that this was a relaxed conversation at a cafe. Clearly he was under pressure; clearly he was very concerned about the trial.'[8] Feldman appeared to have the same view of Ben as the social workers and the psychiatrists, believing that in the lead-up to his death, he did not seem suicidal. Feldman gave me confirmation of this via SMS, having refused a direct interview for this book. Asked whether Ben seemed likely to harm himself, Feldman responded, 'Absolutely not.' He added that Ben was 'not closed inside himself, and he didn't burst into tears. I didn't get the impression that here is a man who is about to take his own life.'

Feldman knows about the profound pressure that comes with extended solitary confinement. He previously represented Israel's most famous segregated prisoner, Mordechai Vanunu, who spent eleven years of an eighteen-year prison sentence in isolation after he used his knowledge as a technician to expose the secrets of Israel's nuclear arsenal in the 1980s. Feldman acknowledged that such prisoners can 'become delusional and lose touch with reality. But I didn't get that sense with Zygier. He was thinking of the future, thinking of his family.'

Feldman also raised an uncomfortable theory favoured by some of Ben's family and friends: that perhaps Ben thought the heavy camera surveillance would enable guards to thwart his suicide attempt, and that he'd then be allowed to move to a less isolated cell. 'It's possible that Ben Zygier was convinced the entire time that the system, which kept him under such close watch, would save him at the last moment,' Feldman said. He added that even as a lawyer with a great deal of jail experience, he hadn't been aware of the extent of camera surveillance in Ben's cell.

Speculation that Ben was somehow killed was aired when a former, unnamed occupant of cell 15 suggested that an attempted suicide could not go unnoticed there. The man gave this earnest analysis in an Israeli television news report:

What worries me was he killed himself, but it's very hard; there's always a camera there. To tear up the sheets, they can see you because they are watching twenty-four hours a day. Even in the night there was a camera with night vision ... So maybe he can do it but it's very hard and I don't know how nobody saw it.[9]

After Ben's death, various conspiracy theories were fuelled by the enforced Israeli secrecy, the concealment that meant the Australian Government received so few details of what was happening to Ben, and which stopped any publication of his story in Israel. But the truth is far more prosaic: the surveillance system in cell 15 was poorly maintained, and the guards knew it.

Out of Focus

In May 2013, I obtain some court documents relating to Ben's death, including summaries from the judge who headed the investigation. Journalists in Israel have already reported from these, but I have had to wait to get them translated from the original Hebrew. I know from past experience that they will contain little nuggets that reporters will have missed or had to exclude because of the pressure of a deadline, so when I finally get the translations, I avidly scan them. What I find are simple but sad facts about the cameras that were relied on to watch over Ben.

Camera number 115 sat above the door on the northern wall of Ben's cell. It broadcast its black-and-white images to the guards in the supervision room next door as well as to the prison's command centre. This camera didn't have much of an area to cover, with the cell measuring just 4 metres by 4 metres—it provided a good view of Ben's bed. Directly opposite it, on the cell's southern wall, was a small transparent door that led to the shower and toilet. The bathroom was beyond the visual range of camera 115, but the door leading into it was captured by camera 116, which sat on the western wall of the cell above the small fridge where Ben was allowed to keep some food. This camera would record crucial black-and-white vision of the shower stall at the time of Ben's death. A third device, camera 117, sat on the eastern wall of the small cell. The only colour camera, it gave a comprehensive wide view of the room, including the fridge and a kitchenette.

Ben may not have been aware of it, but there was a hidden sensor in the centre of the ceiling. A vital but flawed piece of basic technology, it was meant to trigger an infra-red lamp when the cell was in darkness. The type of light emitted by this lamp cannot be seen by the naked eye, but the cameras could, in theory, use it to transmit clear images of the cell once the regular lights were switched off. However, this was not the case in cell 15.

To begin with, the room's trio of cameras were old. Even with the lights on, they provided unfocused, fuzzy images that made monitoring Ben difficult. And the infra-red lamp needed replacement too. At night, the images were so poor that the wardens couldn't see whether Ben was in his bed or in the bathroom. They had to try to decipher 'infinitesimal' differences between dark shadows in the cell. The guards complained about these problems for several months before Ben's death, in particular that, as detailed in the court records, 'when the cell was dark, the visibility was so bad that it was impossible to see what the inmate was doing'. How these cameras were supposed to be used to check on Ben every half-hour is a mystery.

There was a system for reporting such flaws, from a logbook in the guardroom through to a rule that equipment issues had to be reported to the prison's chief technology officer. But Ben's secretive status within the prison defeated these procedures. The man most responsible for Ben's care, Intelligence Officer Ofer, forbade the prison technicians from entering cell 15 to determine whether the cameras could be improved. He concluded that fixing even one of the cameras would take at least half a day and require a technician from the Megason company, which supplied the several hundred other cameras used throughout the prison. Officer Ofer would not entertain the idea of holding Ben elsewhere while the cameras in his cell were taken apart. He allowed that this might be possible if Ben were to be taken to a court or a medical appointment, but the idea was not acted on. Officer Ofer also told the wardens who initially complained that if they wanted any action to be taken, they had to put their concerns down in writing, but no-one did. Neither did Officer Ofer raise the issue with anyone else. The men who ran the prison while Ben was there, two of the most senior officers in Israel's prison service, said they were never told of the camera problems.

Two months before Ben died, however, some action on the shoddy camera issue was taken—but not in Ben's cell. I discover this while reading the court documents. It is a revelation that is both startling and intriguing. For the first time, I come across a reference to cell 13, which apparently was adjacent to Ben's cell and had all of its cameras replaced towards the end of 2010. None of the reportage about Ben had referred to this cell, the existence of which raises the possibility that there might be another Prisoner X. As I make frantic notes about this second isolated cell, I remember how several people in Tel Aviv wondered aloud in my presence whether Ben was the only prisoner kept hidden under a veil of secrecy by Israel. Then I wonder why cell 13 hasn't been mentioned in any newspaper reports, and whether other reporters missed this crucial detail or perhaps are hunting for further information before publishing their speculation.

The guard's complaints were heeded in the case of the cameras in cell 13, and the flaws were repaired. But it seems that the problems in Ben's cell, although significant, were not important enough to override security concerns. One bizarre detail in the court documents is that once the cameras in cell 13 had been replaced, a manager inside the prison said that there was no more money left in the budget to replace any more cameras in that high-security block.

There was one other significant flaw in the surveillance network, and it could have proved crucial on the night Ben died. Camera 116 provided a view of Ben's bathroom—it could be used, for instance, to monitor whether he had entered that room in the middle of the night. But its pictures could only be viewed in the guardroom next door to the cell. The feed from that camera was faulty and was not received in the command centre. That meant that if no-one was in the guardroom, then no-one could see what Ben was doing in his bathroom, or that he had even gone there.

'There were constant complaints about it', one prison guard later said. In fact, all of the guards later said they were aware that most of the inmates who attempted self-harm or suicide did so in the bathroom—it was regarded as a 'hotspot' that required close attention, including from those watching remotely from the command centre. But apparently neither the technology officer on duty nor the officer in overall charge of prison technology knew of camera 116's specific fault. The senior officer said that had he known about it, he would have solved it 'that very day'. This detail is dreadfully vital in regards to Ben's fate, because when he went into his bathroom for the final time, no-one was watching.

Two days before Ben's death, the cameras followed Avigdor Feldman as he left cell 15. The overriding impression Feldman took with him was that one of Ben's biggest fears was that he would be rejected by the Israeli society he had so wanted to join. 'In his heart, Zygier held many cries for help,' Feldman said. 'His life could have been saved.' The genial but big-talking prisoner had migrated to Israel on a wave of ideology, and now he was terrified of living with a tarnished reputation, his name forever associated with betrayal. 'He had been told that he faced very lengthy imprisonment and would be ostracised by his family,' said Feldman. 'That impacts on the soul of a man.'

Diplomacy by the Numbers

Avigdor Feldman's trip to Ayalon coincided with a visit to Israel by one of Australia's best-known politicians. On that Monday, then Foreign Minister Kevin Rudd had a characteristically busy day. After a rapid-fire series of meetings, he travelled to the residence of Israeli President Shimon Peres, took part in a discussion in the office of Prime Minister Benjamin Netanyahu, drove to Ramallah to meet with Palestinian President Mahmoud Abbas, visited a Palestinian girls' school in the West Bank, and finished the day at a formal dinner at the King David Hotel in Jerusalem.

In attendance at that dinner was practically every key person in the relationship between Australia and Israel, including Netanyahu, Cabinet ministers from both countries, some of Australia's wealthiest businessmen, and other people who had made it their life's work to ensure the two countries had close links. It was one of those rare occasions when politicians could talk openly among the professional lobbyists who crowd the periphery of formal diplomacy. Oil could be poured on troubled waters, and new ideas could be proposed. And judging by what was publicly reported at the time, there was much to discuss. Kevin Rudd's recent rhetoric, for instance, was regarded by many in Israel as favouring the Palestinians. Also, the Mossad had quietly shut its station in Canberra after Australia had kicked out Israel's local spy chief. But despite the high-powered nature of the function, and the meetings that had preceded it, nothing turned up on the public record to suggest Ben Zygier was mentioned.

At the time, Ben was in many ways the personification of a key issue over which Israel and Australia genuinely disagreed. But over two years later, Rudd would claim he'd known nothing of Ben's case until the story had broken in the media. Only then would he ask, 'Why was this individual incarcerated by the Israeli authorities?' Had Rudd posed that question while he was in Israel towards the end of 2010, it might have made a very real difference to the fate of Prisoner X. Instead, his speech at the King David Hotel was notable mainly because of a sly dig at one of the more notorious incidents in Israel's history. In 1946, ninety-one people had been killed when the King David Hotel was bombed by an underground Jewish group that included future Israeli prime minister Menachem Begin. The destructive blast gave Rudd his punch line: 'From the 1930s, this hotel became the British field headquarters for what was then British Palestine, until Menachem Begin undertook some interior redesign.'

Foreign Minister Rudd's appointments and comments that day constituted diplomacy by the numbers, although his suggestion that

Israel's nuclear facilities should be opened to international inspectors did create some tension. Rudd was apparently unaware of the irony of raising a subject first exposed by Israel's best-known segregated prisoner, Mordechai Vanunu, while oblivious to the fact that an Australian was now one of Israel's most isolated prisoners.

The next day in Jerusalem, Rudd briefly answered questions from the Australian media, Jason Koutsoukis among them. Then he was driven towards Tel Aviv on the sweeping central freeway that connects many of Israel's busiest centres. A ten-minute detour south of Ben Gurion Airport would have taken Rudd to Ayalon prison. Instead, twenty-six hours before Ben died, Rudd boarded an afternoon flight to London.

In Shadow

Ben woke early on what would be his last day alive, nervous about an upcoming visit by Haya, and turning over in his mind the advice he'd received from Avigdor Feldman. Feldman was not like his current lawyers, Moshe Mazur and others. They had not promised the fierce, anti-establishment advocacy that was Feldman's trademark.

All that year, Ben and his family had felt that if he was just given the opportunity, he might be able to talk his way out of a severe sentence. But Mazur and his colleagues, who had much experience in dealing with the security state, had argued that it was better to cooperate with the process and then try to find the cracks in the evidence, the flaws in the prosecution logic—they favoured securing Ben's innocence by arguing his case. Over the last few months, however, it had become clear that Israel's security state was going to be unrelenting in its quest to punish the former spy. Talking to Feldman had been a concession to this new reality, and now Ben was mulling over the advantages of Feldman's crash-through approach. Feldman had questioned whether they should even concede to the process, a secret court that he believed was illegal. The civil rights lawyer wanted to question the very basis of the hearing, arguing that it had already breached Ben's basic right to have a fair and proper trial.

Ben knew too that Haya was struggling. She'd had to re-establish a home in Israel at short notice and work to calm the children, in particular helping her older daughter adjust to life without her father as a constant presence. Being the wife of an intelligence officer inevitably brought its own pressures, a product of clandestine work involving classified information. But having to deal with a secret arrest, incarceration and trial was an incredible extra burden. Ben knew the tension between them had been growing, but he did not anticipate the stunning news Haya would deliver that day.

According to court documents, Haya was escorted into Ben's cell by a junior intelligence officer at 11.10 a.m. The cameras in his cell captured every moment of Ben's next-to-final conversation with his wife as their five-month-old daughter watched on. But they could not record Haya's exact words or how Ben felt as it dawned on him that his world was radically changing yet again. Nor were the guards listening in, so they couldn't register the full weight of Haya's announcement that she wanted a divorce. For Ben, the news was at first shocking, and ultimately devastating. Assurances were given about maintaining contact with the children, but the family he thought would be waiting for him when he eventually left jail would no longer be there.

Court records revealed that Ben could be seen on the camera footage crumpled with grief. He was so distraught that before Haya left the cell, he forgot to give her a request he'd written out for some warm clothes to help him cope with the coming winter. Ben asked the junior intelligence officer to call Haya back, but the officer refused because it breached the strict rules that governed visits to Ben's cell. Ben's subsequent anger was heard by Haya, who got permission to re-enter Ben's cell, her baby on her hip, to 'try and calm him down'. She spoke with Ben for a few minutes, now in tears herself, and then walked out of the prison, unaware it was the last time she would see her husband alive.

At this time of great vulnerability for Ben, the prison bureau-cracy, a maze of diffuse responsibilities, failed him completely. It was obvious that the prisoner needed extra care, so the junior intelligence officer tried to find someone to ask what he should do. He had previously reported to Intelligence Officer Ofer, but that man had left the prison nine days ago and had passed on very little useful information to his replacement, whom the court records referred to as Officer RA. This man would later claim that after Ben's distress was conveyed to him, he 'immediately' contacted the prison's command centre, which assured him that because Ben was 'upset and nervous, they would devote extra attention [to him], in light of the unusual events of the visit'.

The junior officer would later say he specifically requested that Ben's social worker visit him in his cell, 'to see how he is doing and whether there is something out of the ordinary with him'. He also contacted his former boss, Officer Ofer, who still insisted on knowing everything about Ben even though he no longer worked at Ayalon. Ofer acknowledged in later testimony that on Ben's final day, the prisoner was caught up in 'an emotional storm'. But at the time, he offered the opinion that Ben's disquiet was 'not something unusual or new'.

Ben, deeply upset, contacted the person he always rang, his mother Louise, who was at home in Melbourne. He passed on the devastating news that Haya was leaving him, unable to deal anymore with his situation. He also told his mother that he was considering knocking back the plea bargain offer and taking up Avigdor Feldman's advice to fight back against the system, even if this could potentially increase his final jail term.

According to a family friend, during this conversation, Ben uttered the words, 'I'll see you in the next life'. It was enough to prompt a rapid response from his mother. She sent an email to Ben's lawyer in Israel, Moshe Mazur, writing that she feared Ben would overdose on the sleeping pills he had told her he was stockpiling. Mazur then quickly called Ayalon's command centre and asked to speak with his client, and he spent the next hour talking to Ben. It was another in a series of calls that expressed concern about Ben's welfare to those in charge of the prison. By this stage, the callers believed they had raised enough red flags to ensure Ben would be properly cared for. We now know that belief was misplaced.

Mazur's conversation with Ben later became a point of contention between the Israeli Government and the Zygier family during a court battle over compensation. Mazur's evidence was that the phone call was 'conducted in a calm, quiet and routine manner, and included references to the future'. So the government prosecutor twisted the rhetorical knife and suggested there were few warning signs for the prison staff to act on: 'In complete contrast to the facade he presented, Ben himself never said a word about his suicidal intents. Ben, in a storm of emotions, was probably determined to commit suicide, in contrast to what he openly said in his discussions with the staff and attorney Moshe Mazur.'

It was a wounding statement, made in defence of the prison guards being accused of negligence but personally aimed at the legal team that fought for the Zygier family. An immense burden of guilt tends to accumulate following a suicide, causing its own emotional tumult. But this didn't stop the prosecutor from targeting Mazur's actions on the day of Ben's death, to try to spread the fault widely enough to exonerate Ben's guards. 'Without blaming any of the defence attorneys,' said the prosecutor, 'if they had voiced their clear concerns, then the guards would have and should have increased their supervision. Since they did not speak up, it is another reason that the accumulation of failings discovered in the investigation does not lead to responsibility for negligence.'

It was probably true, though, that those involved in the events of that December day at Ayalon would gladly reconsider what they had done in light of what occurred. Another who was told of Haya's upsetting visit to Ben, but who appeared unconcerned, was the social worker Leila. 'Since this was not the first time that the deceased was upset and crying after telephone conversations and family visits, she [Leila] did not see the storm of emotion as an unusual event and therefore did not give any special instructions,' wrote the investigating judge. Sometime between 5 p.m. and 6 p.m.,

Leila did call the control centre to check on Ben, but she was told by the guards that he was 'calm and watching television'.

Court documents detailed how, at 5.52 p.m., a master sergeant with the initials MA left the supervision room where he had been keeping a close eye on cells 13 and 15. MA was heading into the final hours of a double shift, which he'd requested, and was supposed to stay next to the cells until 10 p.m.. But because the prison was short-staffed that night, he headed back to the command centre, a breach his superior officers regularly approved. However, he left behind the logbook that was supposed to be filled in each half-hour noting observations of Ben. MA's last entry in the logbook read: 'Left the block after locking the cell. No irregularities.'

At 6.05 p.m., Ben switched off the lights in his room and turned on his TV. Camera footage of the cell at that time showed him putting something on a chair near his bed, but the poor-quality image made it difficult to discern. It would turn out to be a bedsheet that Ben had torn into two pieces. A short time later, he turned off his TV.

Around this time, Master Sergeant MA arrived in the guards' small command centre. As he entered, another master sergeant with the initials SA exited. The departing officer was supposed to be in charge of the supervision console in the command centre, monitoring every camera across the prison. But he left for a patrol, in anticipation of a drill that was due to begin at 7 p.m.

At 6.54 p.m. Ben got up from his bed, turned on the TV again and went into his bathroom for the last time. The feed from camera 116 showed Ben standing in the shower stall, mostly in shadow but vaguely illuminated by the glow coming from the TV. But this was the camera in Ben's cell whose images were not relayed to the command centre, just to the adjacent guardroom. So even if the officers in the command centre had been watching the feed from Ben's cell, they would not have seen what transpired.

The footage from camera 116 was indistinct, but it was viewable enough for the investigating judge to describe what happened next:

Despite the extremely poor visibility, when you focus on camera 116 you can see [Ben] doing something for 20 minutes in the location where he hanged himself, and several times you can see the silhouette of a man moving up and down in the same location. The footage is blurry and dark, but since the television set was on, its light helps to show what is happening. Despite the darkness, you can see a man's shadow in the area of the hanging for several minutes without moving. If you view the footage meticulously, you can even see his death throes.

An Empty Bed

At 7.37 p.m., less than twenty minutes after Ben had killed himself, a guard and a medic entered the guardroom beside his cell. But they were not there for Ben. They'd arrived to give some sleeping tablets to the prisoner next door in cell 13. The guard mistakenly noted the visit in the logbook for cell 15: 'Duty medic AAT entered the block to give medical treatment to prisoner D.'

Master Sergeant SA returned to the command centre at 7.40 p.m. It was nearing 8 p.m. when his colleague, MA, noticed that the TV was on in Ben's cell. He was apparently unaware that it had been on for more than an hour (later, Master Sergeant MA would insist that he had checked Ben regularly from about 6 p.m. onwards, but the investigating judge would be sceptical of his testimony). Then MA realised that Ben's bed was empty. But he was not unduly concerned. Instead of checking cell 15 himself, he sent a junior warden to do it instead. At 8.13 p.m., this junior officer noted in the cell's logbook that the inmate was not answering his intercom. He did not enter the cell but summoned MA, who arrived six minutes later and stepped inside. Turning on the light, MA saw Ben in the shower stall, unmoving, the sheet tight around his neck.

MA immediately called for an ambulance and he and the junior officer then tried to resuscitate Ben, but it was too late. The vibrant young Zionist from Melbourne, a man who had been keen to prove he belonged among Israel's elite, had taken his own life.

A series of phone calls then rippled out from the prison, spreading along the interconnected communications web of the security apparatus that had kept Ben's existence a secret. As phones rang in Tel Aviv, members of the prison intelligence service and officers from Shin Bet entered Ben's cell, joining the prison officers and the paramedics. The intelligence officers cleared the room and searched it methodically, making sure that Ben had not left anything behind, either mistakenly or deliberately, that would further compromise the Mossad's operations.

Ben's body was taken from the prison and a doctor was asked to prepare for an autopsy. As dawn broke, news of Ben's suicide was washing up on Haya's front step in Raanana. The Shin Bet had come calling to personally deliver the news that her husband was dead. The agency then phoned Ben's lawyers as well as his parents in Melbourne, and additional calls were made to ASIO and the Department of Foreign Affairs to officially inform the Australian Government. However, for unknown reasons, not a single minister in Julia Gillard's minority Labor government was told about Ben's death.

The International Investigations Unit of Israel's police force, which was often used for sensitive or high-profile cases, was immediately assigned to investigate the suicide. It was problematic that the evidence in Ben's cell was being gathered after it had been examined by the intelligence officers, though the police received an official assurance that no crucial material had been removed.

The first thing the detectives did was take photos and make sketches of Ben's cell, to aid their memories when later presenting evidence and offering explanations to the judge running the inquiry into Ben's death. That inquiry would take many months to complete and would accumulate thick binders full of police files.

ENIGMA

An Unexplained Death

One week after his death, Ben was buried in Springvale, in Melbourne's south-east. His body had been flown back to Australia with the assistance of domestic officials who had little concept of his alleged crimes or where he'd been. The cemetery where he now lies is a grim, soulless place, but it is starkly egalitarian. Jewish cemeteries adhere to strict rules that ensure that every tombstone is the same size—each in the graveyard in Springvale comprises simple black marble engraved with gold lettering. Ben's gravestone, laid several months after he was buried, was inscribed with the Hebrew verse 'May his soul be bounded in the sheaf of life.'

During Ben's funeral, more than 100 people filed past his grave, some throwing a handful of soil on top of his coffin, others using a shovel, fulfilling the Jewish tradition of taking part in the burial. Haya simply accepted condolences, unable to reveal the almost intolerable burden of a husband who was a spy and was jailed in secret, and who killed himself inside a system that no-one is allowed to know about. Over the next few years, she would deal with this burden by drawing together a small circle of friends. Many of the people she'd previously had good relationships with would not understand why they were being shunted aside.

Ben's mother, Louise, who'd heard the distress in her son's voice on the day he'd killed himself, was also in a pit of anguish. Like Haya, deep pain was etched on her face.

Most of those at the funeral had no idea what Ben's job had been, nor did they know how, or where, he had died. The veil of secrecy had billowed out of Israel and had drifted quietly over the gathering of Ben's family and friends in Melbourne. Suicide was clearly implied, but never explained. Traditionally, people who suicide are not permitted to be buried in a Jewish cemetery. Some of his friends felt this was just another reason no one would talk openly about what had happened. Many of the mourners whispered questions to each other: 'Do you know something? Do you know anything?' One person who was there tells me, 'It was awful, especially because it was such a shock … we'd say, "What happened?" And people would reply, "We don't know, he's just dead."'

Some mourners were quietly told that Ben had 'been on a mission that went wrong'. There was also a man at the funeral who publicly addressed those assembled to say that Ben 'had succumbed to the burden' of his responsibilities; although the speaker did not identify his employer, it was widely, and correctly, assumed he was from the Mossad. But the most recent years of Ben's life remained an enigma. One of Ben's closest friends from his life in Melbourne delivered the eulogy, and even he didn't really know what had happened.

One friend says that at the funeral she reflected on the Ben she knew and saw him in a different light. She says it was as if he'd played 'this weird sort of game and then all of a sudden he was dead. It got real when it was too late.'

After the funeral, Haya returned with her daughters to Israel. Ben's parents continued their slow retreat from their friends, while they prayed that Ben's secrets had died with him.

Confusion and Pain

Even though Haya had agreed to an Israeli police investigation, it would be almost a year before she and Ben's parents were told what the police had uncovered, information detailed in bulky binder files and many pages of interview transcripts. The family quickly found lawyers to represent them, but they had to fight through the courts to get access to the police files. And even then, much of the information simply clouded the already hazy picture of Ben's final days and the way he had been treated while under arrest.

The secrecy that had characterised Ben's incarceration continued with the investigation into his death, adding to the family's confusion and pain. They could not tell if this secrecy was the result of an inept bureaucracy, a push to hide any possible negligence, or a need to cover up a more dreadful prospect—that someone had deliberately killed Ben inside the jail.

The official police report contained an autopsy completed four days after Ben's death. It stated he'd been found 'hanging, with a wet, rolled-up sheet held by the bars of the window ... wrapped around his neck'. The verdict of the doctor who'd conducted the autopsy was that 'death was almost certainly caused by mechanical asphyxia by the tightening of a noose around his neck'. There were also some marks on Ben's arm where the skin hadn't been cut and there was no blood. The doctor adjudged that these 'abrasions found on the left forearm were caused by a blunt injury and did not contribute to the death'. It's possible that this is what preoccupied Ben in the twenty minutes when he could be seen moving up and down in the shower stall, testing his makeshift noose and in some way scratching his arm. But the doctor couldn't tell for sure if the abrasions were a result of Ben's suicide attempt or something that had happened prior to it.

The strange marks on Ben's arm, coupled with the substantial lack of access to what the prison officers had told police, added considerably to the Zygier family's fears. They found it hard to dismiss their doubts about whether Ben had really killed himself.

They worried that he may have been cajoled into the act, or drugged, or that there had been some other foul play that was subsequently covered up.

'The family's suspiciousness is understandable,' barrister Roy Blecher explained in court. 'One suspicion includes an intentional act by someone who wanted this death.' Blecher continued:

> There is a mark on the deceased's arm that isn't connected to his suffocation. When a person meets his death by suffocation, there is a possibility that he reached this situation after an argument with someone. So we must ask if there is something in the deceased's corpse that could point to a physical confrontation, something that didn't lead to his death, but that caused him to be choked against his own will.

These concerns were later assuaged by the investigating judge, who'd watched all of the recorded camera feeds from Ben's cell. There were also tests that showed that when he died, Ben had traces of tranquilisers in his blood but no alcohol or narcotics—he hadn't been given any medication on that last day. But the difficulty the family experienced in accessing vital information, stonewalled by a powerful hidden bureaucracy, was a terrible reminder of the system to which Ben had been lost.

A White-hot Story

Nearly two years after Ben's death, his parents approached his gravesite only to discover that a film crew from the ABC was there. Journalist Trevor Bormann and his team, who had been working on Ben's story for months, were just as surprised by the Zygiers' arrival. Geoff Zygier shook Bormann's hand without saying anything. He would later relate the encounter as an example of the media's lack of compassion, explaining that he could not understand how a journalist's job makes them insensitive to a family's concerns. For the Zygiers, the ABC's investigation was the beginning of a second wave of pain.

Bormann had been told about Ben's death by a source in Israel, and he and his producer, Vivien Altman, had been patiently calling anyone they could think of who might help complete the story: those who went to school with Ben, his teachers, his fellow university students. But all had refused to speak to the ABC. Bormann and Altman were surprised by the lack of cooperation. They were the first to discover the implacable resolve of the people clustered around Ben's family. Those who knew the family well had seen the devastation that Ben's death had wrought, and they circled the wagons to keep out the media.

A few weeks after the run-in at the Springvale cemetery, a press release pops up in my email, advertising Bormann's upcoming story on the ABC's *Foreign Correspondent* television program. My interest is sparked by the description of the unnamed Melbourne man who has died in an Israeli jail, but I do not read the email closely. I mention it to the team I work with on ABC Radio as one idea we could broadcast on a Tuesday afternoon, but then I forget to follow it up. The following morning I am making breakfast when Ben's name comes out of the radio during a brief recap of Bormann's story. I am instantly catapulted back in my mind to a school-age Ben Zygier. My mind then flips through the unlikely scenarios that could have led the happy, smiling boy I knew down the path of espionage, imprisonment and death. I rush to the Web, and like everyone else who knew Ben, I'm transfixed by the coverage while trying to correlate the person I knew with the man portrayed in the media.

After the ABC report was aired, links to it and speculation about what happened abounded online. But the mainstream Israeli media were mostly silent. The story had caused a new battle in Israel between its media and its government. Prime Minister Benjamin Netanyahu had swiftly summoned newspaper editors to his office and asked them not to reprint the ABC report, to ensure the nation's 'security' and to save its intelligence agencies from 'embarrassment'. The traditional media then withheld publication because of the onerous court orders that can restrict public discussion of sensitive issues in Israel. However, Ben's death was a white-hot story because this was not about a Palestinian prisoner or a radical protester. Ben could have been any regular Israeli's son or daughter. All the story needed to gain traction were comments from someone inside Israel, quotes that could be published without fear of legal sanction.

Stepping unwittingly into the frame was Justice Minister Yaakov Neeman, who, the day after the ABC story was aired, entered the Israeli Parliament to give his retirement speech. By coincidence, Ben had been held under the legal auspices of Neeman's ministry; the Justice Minister had also helped establish the Tel Aviv law firm that had employed Ben. As Neeman spoke, left-wing politicians began asking questions, aware that they could use the legal immunity provided by the parliament, or Knesset, to get around the strict court orders banning any discussion of Ben's alleged crimes.

One politician who spoke up was Zehava Galon, who was familiar with these kinds of stories. In 2003 she'd helped expose the existence of an interrogation facility called Camp 1391, which she'd called Israel's 'secret Guantanamo Bay'. Now she was determined to pursue the case of Prisoner X. 'We hear that in a country that claims to be a proper democracy, journalists are collaborating with the government, that hidden prisoners commit suicide and no-one knows about their existence,' said Galon. 'How does that sit with proper democracy and the rule of law?'

Soon, other left-of-centre members piled in with their own questions. A representative of the Arab party Ta'al, Ahmed Tibi, asked Neeman if it was true that Zygier had been held in prison under a false name, adding: 'Do you know about the case? Do you confirm the fact that an Australian citizen committed suicide in prison?' Former army spokesman turned politician Nachman Shai pointed out that the Israeli public had already read about Ben's story on websites overseas, 'so it would be better to tell the public the truth, within certain security parameters'. Another Member of Knesset, or MK, Dov Khenin, claimed the aim of the story's suppression was not the protection of national security but rather 'to prevent open public debate'.

Reporters described Neeman as having been 'pummelled' by other politicians during his interrupted speech. Neeman didn't really answer their questions. He just said, 'There is no doubt that if these claims are correct, this has to be checked.' Ultimately, Neeman gave nothing away and helped to shore up the consensus that there was nothing to be gained by discussing Ben's case in public, or at all.

The questions asked by the four MKs attracted a typically ferocious response from one of Israel's most influential right-wing politicians, former foreign minister Avigdor Lieberman: 'These people are trying again and again to harm us, to justify the enemy. They even identify with the enemy in [a] time of war.'[1] Interestingly, the man whose agency had been so successful in keeping Ben's plight secret was unperturbed by the strident questioning by left-leaning politicians. Mossad chief Tamir Pardo reportedly told people inside his agency: 'In a democratic country it's unthinkable to impugn them [the politicians]. We have our job, the courts have their job, and the parliamentarians have their job, and everyone should fulfil their job in good faith.' The quote was carefully planted in Israel's biggest-selling tabloid.[2]

But the story now had its hook, and Israel's feisty media bit down hard. They spent the next few weeks furiously discussing and divulging what had or might have happened, and debating whether there were any more secret prisoners. There were many spurious claims that were repeatedly aired: that Ben might have somehow been killed inside his cell; that he'd been a traitor; that he was a double agent working for Australia. All of these rumours were eventually dismissed, but the people who'd been close to Ben remained glued to the lengthy panel discussions on TV and the updates that burgeoned on internet news sites.

Despite being the spark for this explosion of coverage, the four politicians who'd made that rare breach of political protocol in the Knesset are hard to contact just a few months later. I repeatedly email and call the private offices of Zehava Galon and the others. I speak to their press officers on their mobile phones. I try to make appointments through their Knesset offices. I drive from Tel Aviv to Jerusalem several times, having been told that one MK or another may, just may, be available. But by the time I leave Israel, none of them has spoken with me. All four politicians have refused to speak with me about anything to do with Ben Zygier. One response I receive by email is typical: 'He was very busy. He didn't have time to see your email nor to meet.'

A high degree of trust is evident in Israel's public discussion of the Mossad and those who direct it, so questioning whether the agency deliberately or inadvertently mistreated one of its own was a political risk that was not worth repeating outside of the Knesset. I am told that merely speaking to me, regardless of what is actually said, exposes the politicians to public opprobrium that will only limit their ability to ask such questions in the future. It is an experience I have again and again in pursuing Ben's story. Wherever I go in Israel and Australia, and whomever I talk to, just when I think someone will be willing to talk with me about Ben, a steel gate slams down and stops me in my tracks.

The ensuing months of media coverage took their toll on Ben's family. Many people tell me his parents had just started to emerge from their self-imposed isolation when Ben's story went public in February 2013. They were shocked by the media storm that then engulfed their family name. Such was the exposure—the repeated calls from reporters, the early morning knocks on their door, the pages of newspaper coverage, the repeated images of their son in his army uniform—that in some ways, the media coverage was more confusing and more enraging for Geoff and Louise Zygier than the direct experience of Ben's death.

Suicide is a significant burden for any family, and accepting that Ben had killed himself had caused his parents considerable pain—hurt that had come in the wake of their son's incarceration and the accusations levelled against him. The silence that had then enveloped Ben's Mossad life had only compounded their grief. And when his story was shouted out by the media, the details replayed around the world, they were devastated. Geoff Zygier told one friend that the media exposure had been a searing experience: 'It is like I'm being raped in public.'

The hardest thing about writing this book is knowing the impact it will have on Ben's family, that it will reopen the psychological wounds that they are desperate to heal. But the family's pain is not enough of a reason for me to avoid telling this story. ASIO, the Mossad and the governments of Israel and Australia have simply hidden too much, and this needs to be acknowledged.

When I visit Kibbutz Gazit in May 2013, Rivka Viland lets slip that Haya had sat in her lounge room just a few weeks before my arrival. It is as close as I will get to Ben's elusive wife. Rivka has seen up close the effect on Haya of Ben's secret life and death, and its subsequent portrayal in the media. Sitting in her armchair, she urges me to delay writing this book: 'The parents are distraught. Haya is distraught … Haya needs time with her two girls. She needs years for that before even one of us can, maybe, one evening sit with her and hear her story.'

Rivka says this with an earnestness that is perhaps an echo of what her son has told her—Yoni is still good friends with Haya, which is why I had wanted to speak with him. Rivka then asks me to follow her example: 'We are not pushing. We are not asking questions. It's too early.'

Another Prisoner X

Ben's story was so compelling in Israel because his countrymen couldn't quite believe that this had happened to 'one of us'. The Mossad is trusted and revered, which made the story both shocking and captivating. It was bad enough that someone who had been recruited by this elite organisation had been accused of betraying it, but it was equally remarkable that the agency had then secretly kept the individual behind bars.

While every story eventually fades away, it is clear to me that many people who are close to Israel's politicians and its security agencies believe that Ben was not the only Prisoner X. I am a little surprised by how many people admit to this possibility. 'Could be, could be,' says one of Israel's top broadcasters. The response from civil rights lawyer Michael Sfard is the same: 'This affair makes me almost positive that there are others, especially when no Israeli official has assured the Israeli public that there aren't any other Prisoners X.'

In actual fact, there had been a denial of this. When Ben was first discussed in the Knesset, the Public Security Minister Yitzhak Aharonovitch had answered a question about secret prisoners with a seemingly definitive response: 'There are no anonymous prisoners in Israel.' Yet this is almost certainly not the case. I am shocked when the court documents relating to Ben's case hint at another hidden prisoner in cell 13. (I am also surprised that while the Israeli media had already reported on these documents, seemingly plucking all that was interesting from them, it had not thought this detail worth mentioning.) And more revelations are to come.

The media in Israel eventually lost interest in Ben's case, with only the English-language newspaper *Ha'aretz* persisting with the story. When Ben's parents returned to Israel to fight for compensation for their son's death, it was a *Ha'aretz* reporter, Amir Oren, who pushed for more documents to be released by the court. He kept on doing so even as the Zygier family got closer and closer to resolving their legal battle with the Israeli Government, and he was eventually successful. The documents do not reveal why Ben's family accepted compensation and agreed to stop any further court action against their son's jailers and his former employer. Many of Ben's friends asked why his family did not ask for more help from the Australian Government when Ben was alive, and why the family decided to stop fighting his cause in court. There are rumours that the compensation package includes an agreement not to talk to the media, as well as to discontinue court action, but it remains a mystery to me why his family did not call on the Jewish community's considerable political connections in Canberra and Tel Aviv to argue their son's case more forcefully. For reasons I have been unable to uncover, his family have done whatever they can to suppress any discussion or mention of their son's story.

What these documents do reveal is that Ben's case was not an isolated one, but that he was part of a system that hid the detention of intelligence operatives from the Israeli public. There appeared to be at least one other prisoner in this system, someone who had been in jail for an unknown number of years. And according to Avigdor Feldman, his case was 'far more sensational, far more astounding and far more fascinating' than Ben Zygier's. Most Israelis didn't seem too concerned by what they learned. But MK Zehava Galon again hit out at the government, referring to the Public Security Minister's previous claim that no more prisoners were being held incognito: 'In a democracy, there cannot be secret prisoners, with no outside supervision of where and under what conditions they are held. In a democracy, ministers do not lie to the Knesset and the public.' She later said that the government minister's behaviour was 'befitting of a totalitarian state'.

Amir Oren published an online article about this second Prisoner X, which was soon taken down by the Israeli military censors. In the article, Oren claimed this prisoner had once been an intelligence agent, likely for the Mossad, and that he'd travelled around the world. He said the prisoner was married and that his wife visited him regularly. Subsequently, Avigdor Feldman did a media interview blitz during which he reasserted that both Ben and this second Prisoner X had worked for intelligence agencies, and that in both cases 'their activity points to a security failure that allowed the crime to be committed and secrets to be kept'. Even in death, Ben was still being used as a yardstick for how far the state would go to cover up the mistakes of its own top-secret operatives.

In a follow-up story that was also quickly taken offline by the censors, Oren alleged that the second Prisoner X, unlike Ben, had submitted himself to some sort of secret trial and might have his sentence reduced by one-third for good behaviour. The article claimed that the investigators looking into the prisoner's crimes had conducted interviews with hundreds of people, and that it had been the toughest case ever faced by the detective assigned to it. It described the sort of investigation Ben might have endured had he lived.

According to Feldman, the case of the second Prisoner X was even more worrying than Ben's: 'This affair points to far more severe failures than the ones committed by the defense establishment in Zygier's case.' Describing the types of violations the other Prisoner X allegedly committed, Feldman suggested those in charge of this agent had been much more complicit in giving him the leeway to commit his crime. 'It's a horrible security breach,' Feldman claimed. 'We are talking about secrets that if revealed will harm not only the security of the state, but primarily those organisations and their senior commanders who would lose their jobs.'

Greater Justice

We will never know what Ben's state of mind was in the last few years of his life, let alone the last few minutes. The charges against him may never be revealed, and even if they are, we will never know if he would have been found guilty or innocent; nor are we likely to see any record of his defence of his own conduct.

Ben's family eventually settled with the Israeli Government, securing a A$1.2 million payment in exchange for agreeing not to pursue a civil case for compensation. Geoff Zygier may have received some answers to his many questions about his son when he met with Prime Minister Benjamin Netanyahu in 2012. The investigating judge in Ben's case said the prison service in general, and some officers in particular, should face charges of negligence. But the decision was left in the hands of the state prosecutor and no charges were laid against the officers.

Intelligence Officer Ofer told the police detectives who investigated Ben's suicide that he'd been a mere functionary. The police clearly came to the conclusion that this officer bore most of the responsibility for the procedures that governed Ben's life. But Ofer avoided accepting this responsibility, acidly telling his interrogators that Ben's cell was only one part of the prison and that 'I have yet to be appointed manager of Ayalon.'

How was someone potentially so unstable given responsibility inside the Mossad? It has subsequently said it has tightened its recruitment procedures, in the hope of avoiding a repeat of the mistakes it admitted it made with Ben Zygier.

Why wasn't Ben given more support and why did his incarceration cause such little concern inside the Australian Government? Why was it kept outside the normal diplomatic channels, and why was his arrest never raised in the context of the hit in Dubai?

Australia might one day face another case like Ben Zygier's. I'm told by someone with extensive national security experience that 'the dual national issue is a problem we have to do something about'. As we sit in a cafe near one of ASIO's offices, this person tells me there is no easy answer to the often-asked question of how you handle dual nationals who end up working for foreign intelligence agencies. The Australian Government's diplomats and intelligence agencies do not have a simple way of ensuring that Australian passports are not misused by a foreign power. They have no straightforward rules to follow if an Australian citizen is targeted or arrested while working as a spy for another nation. It's still not clear what obligations Australia would have if such a scenario were repeated—there would again be question marks over whether to visit the Australian in jail, whether to help defend them in court, or whether Canberra should make a plea on their behalf. 'It is a genuine concern,' says my national security source. 'We don't have any clear answers.'

By now, the second Prisoner X may well have been moved on from Ayalon, but it is impossible to know because Israel's prisoner service obviously won't confirm or deny this. The high-security cellblock now has 24-hour-a-day supervision and its cameras have been upgraded. So it's likely this second prisoner continues to pace up and down a private courtyard at Ayalon, watched more closely as a result of Ben's suicide.

We still don't know how many Israelis care about this secret prison system and the legal process that covertly condemns people to years behind bars. There has been little public debate about this. Some civil rights lawyers tell me that every member of the Israeli Knesset has the legal right to enter any prison cell and examine the conditions an inmate is being held under. But this is not a legal right that any Israeli politician has yet chosen to exercise. And it's not hard to guess why. In an article that no longer exists online, an anonymous contributor familiar with the second Prisoner X case summed up the dominant attitude when Israelis ponder the fate of spies who deliberately or inadvertently betray their country's vital secrets: 'He deserves a bullet in his brain.'

It's likely that few Israelis believe that Ben deserved to die, but most seem to be willing to allow their government to punish its own, in secret. We need to ask why such secrets are kept, how such negligence can occur inside two modern, thriving democracies, and why no one is being held accountable. Next time, maybe the trial will be just a little less secret. Perhaps a little more transparency will bring greater justice.

ACKNOWLEDGEMENTS

To Monk Bodhi Dharma, Common Ground and Dukes, thanks for the coffee. Thank you to Nick McKenzie, who has taught me so much, to Jonathan Harley for being there, to Thom Cookes for his constant willingness to listen and read, to Sally Health for her skill and talent as an editor, to Paul Smitz for his remarkable editing and to Louise Adler for her support.

This book could not have been written without the journalism that came before it, especially that of Trevor Bormann and Vivien Altman at the ABC and Amir Oren at *Ha'aretz*. I would also like to acknowledge the years of good work produced by Ronen Bergman, Jason Koutsoukis and Yossi Melman. I also drew from the work of national security journalists in the United States like David Sanger.

My thanks to ABC Radio, especially to MJ. Finally, behind every writer is an exhausted family. Thank you to my wider family for their unstinting support. Most importantly, none of my work outside my family home would be possible without the love of my sons and my wife. You are my inspiration and my joy.

NOTES

Author's Note

1   Dan Raviv and Yossi Melman (2012), *Spies against Armageddon: Inside Israel's Secret Wars*, Levant Books.

A Dark Day

1   www.ynetnews.com/articles/0,7340,L-4345279,00.html
2   Ibid.

Boy

1   Orthodox Jews don't write down the word 'God' in full in case the paper it is printed on is later destroyed.

Student

1   http://972mag.com/hagai-amir-i-dont-regret-rabins-murder-because-you-cant-regret-mitzvah/55027/

Soldier

1   www.haaretz.com/news/diplomacy-defense/australian-born-mossad-prisoner-lived-as-lone-soldier-on-kibbutz.premium-1.503354

Spy

1   Dan Raviv and Yossi Melman (2012), *Spies against Armageddon: Inside Israel's Secret Wars*, Levant Books, p. 308.
2   Ibid., p. 314.
3   www.spiegel.de/international/world/how-the-mossad-career-of-ben-zygier-ended-in-treason-a-890854-2.html
4   David E Sanger (2012), *Confront and Conceal: Obama's Secret Wars and Surprising Use of American Power*, Broadway Books, p. 194.
5   Ibid.
6   Ibid.

Suspect

1 www.haaretz.com/news/diplomacy-defense/friend-of-prisoner-x-mossad-made-big-mistake-recruiting-zygier.premium-1.506642
2 www.wired.com/threatlevel/2012/04/shady-companies-nsa/all/1

Prisoner

1 www.theage.com.au/national/ben-zygier-asio-suspect-who-died-in-israeli-jail-20130213-2edid.html
2 Dan Raviv and Yossi Melman (2012), *Spies against Armageddon: Inside Israel's Secret Wars*, Levant Books, p. 282.
3 http://www.gq.com/news-politics/big-issues/201101/the-dubai-job-mossad-assassination-hamas
4 http://www.cablegatesearch.net/cable.php?id=10DUBAI29
5 Ibid.
6 www.aljazeera.com/focus/2010/02/2010271441269105.html
7 Paul McGeough (2010), *Kill Khalid: The Failed Mossad Assassination of Khalid Mishal and the Rise of Hamas*, New Press.
8 www.spiegel.de/international/world/a-pandora-s-box-arrest-of-suspected-mossad-agent-strains-german-israeli-relations-a-701826.html
9 http://foreignminister.gov.au/releases/2013/bc_mr_130305.html
10 http://foreignminister.gov.au/releases/2013/bc_mr_130305.html (part 12 of attachment B)
11 www.abc.net.au/am/content/2010/s2829614.htm
12 www.smh.com.au/world/australian-passports-used-in-dubai-attack-20100225-p3tn.html
13 www.theaustralian.com.au/news/joshua-daniel-bruce-passport-photo-is-not-my-son-mother/story-e6frg6n6-1225834396361
14 www.news.com.au/national/meet-australian-woman-nicole-mccabe-set-up-in-spy-scandal/story-e6frfkvr-1225834556008

Prisoner X

1 Dan Raviv and Yossi Melman (2012), *Spies against Armageddon: Inside Israel's Secret Wars*, Levant Books, p. 310.
2 http://foreignminister.gov.au/transcripts/2010/100525_sky_news.html

3   www.smh.com.au/national/australia-forges-passports-too-says-bishop-20100525-wa6b.html
4   http://www.sciencemedia.com.au/downloads/2013-3-10-2.pdf
5   Ibid.
6   http://foreignminister.gov.au/transcripts/2013/bc_tr_130603_press_conference.html
7   Dan Raviv and Yossi Melman (2012), *Spies against Armageddon: Inside Israel's Secret Wars*, Levant Books, and author interview with Yossi Melman.
8   www.timesofisrael.com/attorney-met-with-prisoner-x-just-before-his-death/
9   http://www.abc.net/7.30/content/2013/53710167.htm

Enigma

1   http://maki.org.il/en/?p=734
2   http://www.timesofisrael.com/attorney-met-with-prisoner-x-just-before-his-death

INDEX